LEARNING
FROM
GREAT
SCIENTISTS

LEARNING FROM GREAT SCIENTISTS

THE POWER OF ASKING WHY

Vitasta Originals

Published by

Renu Kaul Verma

Vitasta Publishing Pvt Ltd

4348/4C, Ansari Road, Daryaganj

New Delhi - 110 002

info@vitastapublishing.com

 an imprint of Vitasta Publishing

ISBN: 978-81-19670-07-9
© Vitasta Publishing
First Edition 2025

MRP ₹ 395

Layout & Cover Design by Rohit Gautam

Printed by Vikas Computer and Printers, New Delhi

Contents

Publisher's Note

At Vitasta Publishing, we believe that the spirit of discovery is one of humanity's greatest gifts. *Learning from Great Scientists: The Power of Asking Why* captures this spirit beautifully, offering young readers a bridge between the groundbreaking achievements of history's greatest minds and their own boundless potential.

Through vivid storytelling, this collection introduces children to the lives and works of renowned figures such as Archimedes, Jagadish Chandra Bose, Alan Turing, Marie Curie, and Rachel Carson. More than a chronicle of scientific milestones, this book is a tribute to the power of curiosity, perseverance, and imagination—qualities that define every great scientist, and every great learner.

We are proud to present *Learning from Great Scientists* as an inspiring companion for classrooms, libraries, and homes everywhere, encouraging children to see the wonder of the world through the eyes of those who changed it forever—and to imagine how they might one day do the same.

Foreword

Curiosity is inherent in children and it is also a quality that good scientists have. This little book explores the wonderful world of science through the curious eyes of children, encouraged and supported by loving parents, grandparents and teachers. All the living legends of science, pictured in this book, like Wilhelm Conrad Röntgen, Alan Turing, William Perkin, Hypatia, J C Bose, Marie Curie, Rosalind Franklin and so many others, were once curious children. This is why they turned to science. Science is about finding out about the world around us, why stars twinkle in the night, why the sky is blue, why the monsoon comes only after summer, why sugar is sweet, why a light bulb glows: in fact, science is all about getting to know more about anything and everything we see, hear, smell, feel and touch. This book tells children that science is not about getting grades in exams but about knowing more about the world and in the end about themselves. Better science makes for better living and the seeds of science are best sown in young minds. This is why I congratulate Vitasta Publications for bringing out *Learning from Great Scientists* and warmly recommend it to both young and not so young readers.

Professor Gautam R Desiraju
Indian Institute of Science, Bengaluru

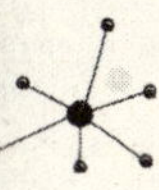
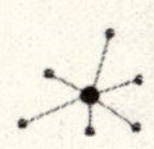

Jagadish Chandra Bose
Crescograph

Eunice Newton Foote
Greenhouse effect

Mikhail Dolivo-Dobrovolsky
Three-phase electric power

Archimedes
Buoyancy principle;
simple machines

Michael Faraday
Electromagnetic induction

Charles Goodyear
Vulcanized rubber

Samuel Morse
Morse code; telegraph

Rachel Carson
Environmental impact of pesticides

Thomas Edison
Practical electric light bulb;
phonograph

William Perkin
Synthetic dye (mauve)

Hypatia
Commentary on geometry and astronomy

Mary Anning
Fossil discoveries (ichthyosaur, plesiosaur)

Edmond Becquerel
Photovoltaic effect

Charles F Brush
Arc lamp; wind-powered
generator

Katherine Johnson
Spaceflight trajectory
calculations

Alan Turing
Codebreaking;
foundations of computing

Wilhelm Conrad Röntgen
Discovery of X-rays

Jan Ingenhousz
Photosynthesis (plants release
oxygen in sunlight)

Erwin Schrödinger
Schrödinger equation;
quantum theory

Rosalind Franklin
DNA double helix (X-ray crystallography)

James Watt
Improved steam engine

Euclid
Foundations of geometry
(Elements)

Jacques Cousteau
Aqua-Lung; ocean exploration
and conservation

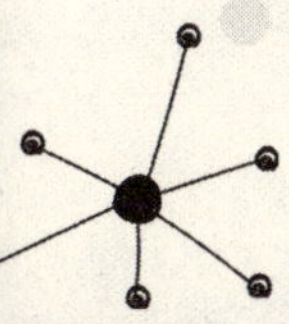

Jagadish Chandra Bose
Invention: Crescograph

Jagadish Chandra Bose was a famous Indian scientist who lived from 1858 to 1937. He was one of the first people to show that plants can feel and respond to their surroundings. He invented special instruments to measure how plants react to things like light, heat, and touch. He also worked with radio waves and made important discoveries in wireless communication, even before other well-known scientists.

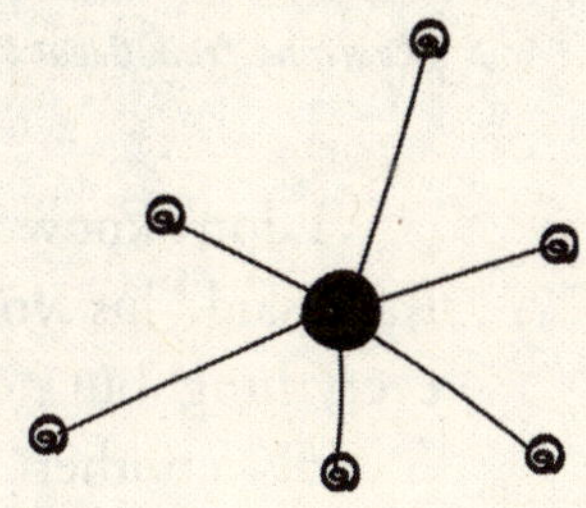

Ravi's Green Discovery

Ravi sat at his desk, staring at the blank sheet of paper in front of him. The deadline for his science project for the school science fair was just a week away, and he still hadn't come up with an idea. His classmates had already started working on their projects—some were building miniature volcanoes, others were creating solar-powered cars, and a few were even experimenting with chemical reactions. But Ravi? He had nothing. The more he thought about it, the more his stomach churned with anxiety.

'What if I get zero marks?' he muttered to himself, running his fingers through his hair. 'I'll be the only one in class with no project. Everyone will laugh at me.'

His mother walked into the room, carrying a plate of sliced fruit. She noticed the worry etched on her son's face and sat down beside him. 'Ravi, what's wrong? You've been sitting here for hours.'

'I don't know what to do for my science project, Ma,' Ravi said, his voice trembling. 'I've tried thinking of everything, but nothing comes to mind. What if I fail?'

His mother placed a comforting hand on his shoulder. 'You're overthinking it, *beta*. Sometimes, the best ideas come when you least expect them. Why don't you take a break? Go visit your grandfather. He always has interesting stories to tell. Maybe he'll inspire you.'

Ravi sighed. 'I don't know how Dada's stories will help me with a science project, but I guess it's better than sitting here and doing nothing.'

The next morning, Ravi packed a small bag and headed to his grandfather's house, which was a short bus ride away. His grandfather, a retired schoolteacher, lived in a cosy little cottage surrounded by a lush garden. As Ravi approached the house, he saw his grandfather tending to the plants, humming a tune.

'Dada!' Ravi called out, waving.

His grandfather looked up and smiled. 'Ah, Ravi! What a pleasant surprise. Come, come, let's sit inside. I'll make us some tea.'

Once they were settled in the living room, Ravi's grandfather handed him a steaming cup of tea. 'So, what brings you here today? You look troubled, son.'

Ravi hesitated for a moment before pouring out his worries. 'Dada, I have to make a science project for school, but I can't think of anything. I'm scared I'll fail.'

His grandfather chuckled softly. 'Science projects can be daunting, but they're also an opportunity to explore and learn. Tell me, what do you find interesting about science?'

Ravi shrugged. 'I don't know. I like plants, I guess. But I don't see how I can make a project out of that.'

His grandfather's eyes twinkled with excitement. 'Plants, you say? Ravi, have you ever heard of Jagadish Chandra Bose?'

Ravi frowned. 'Jagadish Chandra Bose? Wasn't he a scientist, Dada?'

'Yes, and a brilliant one at that,' his grandfather replied. 'He was one of the first scientists to prove that plants have life. In fact, he invented a device called the Crescograph to measure their growth.'

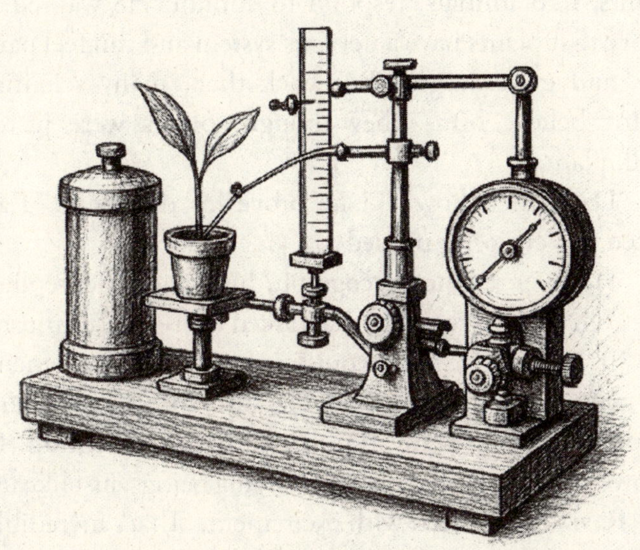

Crescograph

Ravi's eyes widened. 'Plants have life? And there's a device to measure their growth? That sounds… amazing.'

His grandfather leaned back in his chair, a nostalgic smile on his face. 'Let me tell you more about him.'

Ravi's interest piqued and he started getting ideas regarding his science project.

'Jagadish Chandra Bose was born in 1858 in Bengal. He was a polymath—a person who excelled in multiple fields. He studied physics, biology, and even wrote science fiction books. But what made him truly remarkable was his curiosity and determination.'

'What did he do?' Ravi asked, leaning forward.

'Well,' his grandfather began, 'Bose believed that plants, like animals, respond to stimuli. He wanted to prove that plants have a nervous system and can feel pain, joy, and even fatigue. But back then, many scientists didn't believe him. They thought plants were just… well, plants.'

'Dada then how did he prove his discovery?' Ravi asked, his curiosity piqued

'He invented the crescograph,' his grandfather replied.

'What's a crescograph?' Ravi asked with earnest curiosity.

'It is a device that could magnify the movements of plants, allowing him to measure their growth and responses to different stimuli. With this invention, he showed the world that plants are living beings, just like us.'

Ravi's mind raced with excitement. 'That's incredible! But how did the crescograph work?'

'Ah, that's the fascinating part,' his grandfather said.

'The crescograph used a series of levers and a smoked glass plate to record even the tiniest movements of plants. Bose would expose plants to different conditions—like light, heat, or chemicals—and observe how they reacted. His experiments proved that plants have a lifeforce, just like animals.'

Ravi's eyes sparkled with inspiration. 'Dada, do you think I could make a project about the crescograph? Maybe I could build a simple version of it and show how it works.'

His grandfather beamed. 'That's a wonderful idea, Ravi! You could explain how Bose's invention changed the way we understand plants. And who knows? Maybe you'll inspire your classmates to see plants in a new light.'

***

Over the next few days, Ravi threw himself into his project. With his grandfather's guidance, he built a simple crescograph using materials they found around the house—a magnifying glass, a lever, and a piece of smoked glass. He set up an experiment with a potted plant, exposing it to different conditions and recording its growth.

On the day of the science fair, Ravi stood proudly beside his project, a poster explaining Jagadish Chandra Bose's work and a live demonstration of his homemade crescograph. His classmates gathered around, fascinated by the tiny movements of the plant magnified on the smoked glass.

'This is so cool, Ravi!' one of his friends exclaimed. 'I never knew plants could move like that.'

Ravi grinned, pleased with their reaction. 'Yeah, it's pretty mind—blowing, right?' he said, brushing a leaf gently with his fingertip. 'It's like they have their own secret world.'

'Totally,' another chimed in, nodding thoughtfully. 'And Jagadish Chandra Bose—wow, he sounds like an amazing scientist. I had no idea he did all that stuff. I'm definitely going to read more about him.'

When the judges came by, Ravi explained his project with confidence.

'Jagadish Chandra Bose's work showed us that plants are living beings, just like us. His invention, the crescograph, helped us understand how plants respond to their environment. I wanted to share his story because it reminds us that science is about curiosity and discovery.'

The judges were impressed. 'This is a unique and well-researched project, Ravi,' one of them said. 'You've done an excellent job.'

When the results were announced, Ravi's project won first prize. As he stood on the stage, holding his trophy, he felt a surge of pride and gratitude. He knew he couldn't have done it without his grandfather's guidance and the inspiring story of Jagadish Chandra Bose.

That evening, Ravi returned to his grandfather's house to share the good news. 'Dada, I won! My project won first prize!'

His grandfather hugged him tightly. 'I knew you could do it, Ravi. I'm so proud of you.'

As they sat together in the garden, surrounded by the plants that had inspired his project, Ravi felt a deep sense of fulfillment. He realised that science wasn't just about getting good grades—it was about exploring the wonders of the world and sharing those discoveries with others. And thanks to his grandfather and Jagadish Chandra Bose, he had found his passion.

'Dada,' Ravi said, looking at the plants swaying gently in the breeze, 'I think I want to be a scientist when I grow up. I want to discover new things, just like Jagadish Chandra Bose.'

His grandfather smiled. 'Then you'll be a great one, Ravi. Just remember to stay curious and never stop asking questions.'

And with that, Ravi's journey into the world of science had only just begun.

Over the next few weeks, Ravi's fascination with plants and science grew. He spent hours in the school library, reading about Jagadish Chandra Bose and his other inventions. He learned about Bose's contributions to radio waves and his pioneering work in biophysics. Ravi was amazed by how one man could have such a profound impact on so many fields of science.

One day, his science teacher, Mrs Kapoor, noticed his newfound enthusiasm. 'Ravi, you've been spending a lot of time in the library. What are you reading?'

'I've been learning about Jagadish Chandra Bose,

ma'am,' Ravi replied. 'His work on plants and radio waves is incredible. Did you know he was the first to use semiconductor junctions to detect radio waves?'

Mrs Kapoor smiled. 'I did, actually. He was a true visionary. It's wonderful to see you taking such an interest in his work. Have you thought about doing another project on him?'

Ravi's eyes lit up. 'Ma'am, I was thinking about building a simple radio receiver, like the ones Bose used in his experiments. Do you think that would be a good idea?'

'Absolutely,' Mrs Kapoor said. 'It's a challenging project, but I think you're more than capable of pulling it off. Let me know if you need any help.'

With Mrs Kapoor's encouragement, Ravi began working on his new project. He spent weekends at his grandfather's house, tinkering with wires, crystals, and coils. His grandfather, who had a knack for electronics, guided him through the process.

'Remember, Ravi,' his grandfather said, 'Science is about trial and error. Don't be afraid to make mistakes. That's how you learn.'

After weeks of hard work, Ravi finally completed his radio receiver. He brought it to school to show Mrs Kapoor and his classmates. As he demonstrated how it could pick up radio signals, everyone was amazed.

'This is incredible, Ravi!' one of his classmates said. 'You're like a young Jagadish Chandra Bose!'

Ravi blushed. 'I still have a lot to learn, but I'm really

enjoying it. Science is so much fun when you're curious and willing to explore.'

Mrs Kapoor nodded approvingly. 'You've come a long way, Ravi. I'm proud of you.'

As the school year came to an end, Ravi reflected on how much he had grown. He had started the year feeling lost and unsure, but now he had a clear sense of direction. He knew he wanted to pursue a career in science, just like his idol, Jagadish Chandra Bose.

One evening, as he sat in his grandfather's garden, Ravi looked up at the stars and smiled. 'Dada, do you think I'll ever make a discovery as big as Bose's?'

His grandfather chuckled. 'Who knows, Ravi? The world of science is full of possibilities. If you stay curious and work hard, there's no limit to what you can achieve.'

Ravi nodded, feeling a sense of peace and determination. He knew the road ahead wouldn't be easy, but he was ready to face the challenges. With the memory of Jagadish Chandra Bose's legacy guiding him, he felt confident that he could make a difference in the world of science.

And so, Ravi's journey continued, fueled by curiosity, passion, and the unwavering support of his grandfather. As he looked to the future, he knew that the wonders of science were waiting to be discovered—and he was ready to explore them all.

Eunice Newton Foote

Discovery: Greenhouse Effect

Eunice Newton Foote was an American scientist, inventor, and women's rights activist who lived from 1819 to 1888. She conducted groundbreaking experiments in 1856 that demonstrated how carbon dioxide and water vapour could trap heat in the atmosphere. Her work was among the earliest to suggest the Greenhouse Effect, a concept that is central to modern climate science.

Today, Eunice Newton Foote is increasingly recognised as a pioneer whose early work laid important foundations for both climate science and the fight for women's rights.

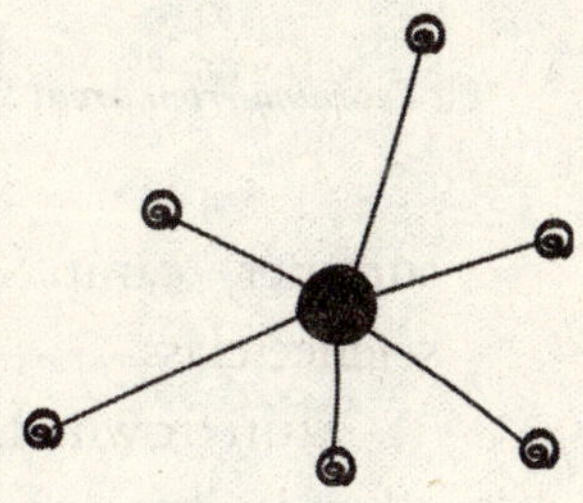

Stuti and the Greenhouse Effect

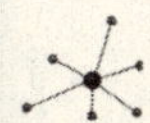

The sun was high in the sky, casting a golden glow over the sprawling grounds of the summer camp. Stuti sat on the steps of her cabin, her chin resting on her hands, staring at the piece of paper in her lap. It was their first day at camp, and the group leaders had already assigned them a science project.

The task?

Prove the greenhouse effect.

Stuti groaned. 'The greenhouse effect? How are we supposed to do that? It sounds so complicated!'

Her friends, Priyanka and Neha, sat beside her, looking equally worried. Priyanka, the practical one, flipped through the instructions. 'It says here we have to demonstrate how certain gases trap heat in the atmosphere. But how do we even start?'

Neha, the dreamer of the group, sighed. 'I thought

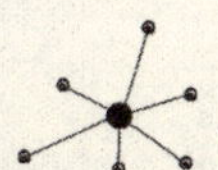

summer camp was supposed to be fun. Not… science class.'

Stuti frowned. 'I don't even know what the greenhouse effect is, do you?'

Priyanka shook her head. 'Not really. Something about the Earth getting warmer because of gases, I think.'

Neha groaned. 'This is impossible. We're going to fail, and everyone will laugh at us.'

Stuti bit her lip. She hated the idea of failing, especially in front of the other campers. But she also didn't know where to begin. 'Maybe we should ask for help,' she suggested.

'From who?' Priyanka asked. 'The group leaders? They'll just tell us to figure it out ourselves.'

'Not the group leaders,' Stuti said. 'What about that senior camper we met earlier? The one with the glasses and the notebook? She seemed really smart.'

Neha's eyes lit up. 'Oh, you mean Ananya? Yeah, she's always doing experiments and stuff. Maybe she can help us.'

The three girls quickly packed up their things and set off to find Ananya. They found her near the campfire pit, scribbling notes in her notebook. She looked up as they approached. 'Hey, what's up?'

Stuti hesitated for a moment before blurting out, 'We need help with our science project. We have to prove the greenhouse effect, but we don't even know where to start.'

Ananya smiled. 'Ah, the greenhouse effect. That's a cool topic. Do you know that the first person to prove it was a woman named Eunice Newton Foote?'

Stuti's eyes widened. 'Really? I've never heard of her.'

'Most people haven't,' Ananya said. 'She was a scientist in the 1800s, long before climate change became a big topic. She did an experiment with glass cylinders and different gases to show how carbon dioxide traps heat. It was groundbreaking work, but she didn't get much credit for it at the time.'

Priyanka leaned forward, intrigued. 'What kind of experiment did she do?'

Ananya explained, 'She filled glass cylinders with different gases—like carbon dioxide, oxygen, and air—and placed them in the sun. Then she measured how much each gas heated up. She found that carbon dioxide got the hottest, proving that it traps heat more than other gases.'

Neha's eyes sparkled. 'That sounds like something we could do! Do you think we could recreate her experiment?'

Ananya nodded. 'Absolutely. You'd need some glass jars, a thermometer, and a way to measure the temperature. It's simple but effective.'

Stuti felt a surge of hope. 'That doesn't sound too hard. Do you think the camp has the materials we need?'

'Probably,' Ananya said. 'I'll help you gather everything. Let's get started.'

***

The next morning, Stuti, Priyanka, and Neha met Ananya at the camp's storage shed. They collected four glass jars, a thermometer, and some baking soda and vinegar to create carbon dioxide. Ananya also helped them find a sunny spot near the edge of the camp where they could set up their experiment.

'Okay,' Ananya said, 'let's label the jars. One will have regular air, one will have oxygen, one will have carbon dioxide, and the last one will be empty as a control.'

Stuti carefully filled the jars according to Ananya's instructions. For the carbon dioxide jar, she mixed baking soda and vinegar, capturing the gas that bubbled up. Priyanka placed the thermometer inside each jar, while Neha recorded the starting temperatures.

'Now we just have to wait,' Ananya said. 'Check the temperature every 10 minutes and write it down.'

As the sun rose higher in the sky, the girls watched intently. Stuti couldn't help but feel a little nervous. What if the experiment didn't work? What if they had done something wrong?

After an hour, Neha compared the temperatures. 'Look at this!' she exclaimed. 'The carbon dioxide jar is way hotter than the others. It's just like Eunice Newton Foote's experiment!'

Stuti grinned. 'It worked! We actually proved the greenhouse effect!'

Priyanka high-fived her. 'I can't believe it. It was so simple, but it makes so much sense.'

Ananya smiled proudly. 'You guys did a great job. Now you just have to present your findings to the group leaders.'

***

The next day, Stuti, Priyanka, and Neha stood in front of their group, ready to present their project. Stuti held up the jars and explained the experiment. 'We recreated Eunice Newton Foote's experiment to prove the greenhouse effect. We filled these jars with different gases and measured how much they heated up in the sun. The jar with carbon dioxide got the hottest, showing that it traps heat more than other gases.'

She pointed to the thermometer readings Neha had recorded. 'As you can see, the carbon dioxide jar's temperature increased significantly, while the others stayed relatively cool. This demonstrates how carbon dioxide in the atmosphere traps heat, contributing to the greenhouse effect.'

The group leaders were visibly impressed. 'This is an excellent project,' one of them said. 'You not only proved the greenhouse effect but also highlighted the work of an often-overlooked scientist. Well done!'

The other campers clapped, and Stuti felt a rush of pride. She glanced at Priyanka and Neha, who were beaming. They had done it—they had completed the project and even learned something new in the process.

After the presentation, Stuti found Ananya and thanked her. 'We couldn't have done it without you. You made it so easy to understand.'

Ananya smiled. 'You guys did all the work. I just pointed you in the right direction. Remember, science is about curiosity and teamwork. You proved that today.'

As the sun set over the camp, Stuti sat with her friends by the campfire, feeling a sense of accomplishment. She had started the week feeling scared and unsure, but now she felt confident and inspired. Thanks to Eunice Newton Foote's groundbreaking work and Ananya's guidance, she had discovered the joy of science.

'You know,' Stuti said, 'I think I want to learn more about climate change and how we can help the planet. Maybe I'll even become a scientist one day.'

Priyanka grinned. 'I'll be your lab partner.'

Neha laughed. 'And I'll make sure you two don't blow anything up.'

As the fire crackled and the stars twinkled above, Stuti felt a sense of excitement for the future. She knew there was so much more to learn and discover, and she was ready to take on the challenge.

Mikhail Dolivo-Dobrovolsky

Invention: Three-phase electric power system

Mikhail Dolivo-Dobrovolsky was a Russian-born engineer and inventor who lived from 1862 to 1919. He is best known for his major contributions to the development of Alternating Current (AC) electrical systems. While working in Germany, he designed the three-phase electric power system, which is still used around the world today to transmit electricity efficiently over long distances.

He also invented the three-phase induction motor, an important part of many machines and appliances we use every day.

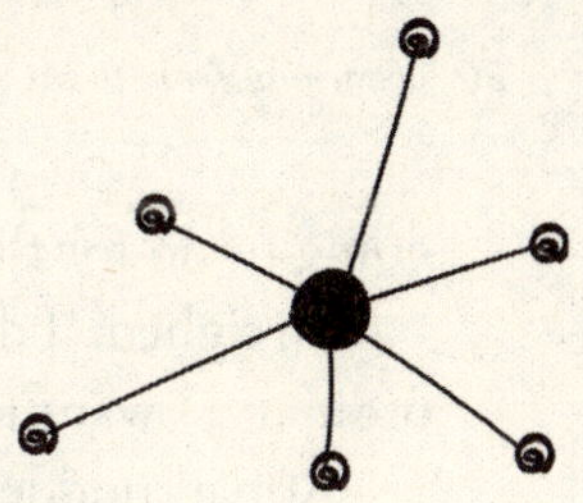

Jai and the AC Motor

Jai sat at his desk, staring at the blank page in front of him. The classroom buzzed with excitement as his classmates discussed their ideas for the upcoming Science Week assignment. The theme was 'The Biggest Science Discoveries and Inventions in History,' and everyone seemed to have a plan—except Jai.

His rival, Veer, was already sketching diagrams of Thomas Edison's light bulb. 'I'm going to make a working model,' Veer boasted, loud enough for Jai to hear. 'It's going to be the best project in the class.'

Thomas Edison's light bulb.

Jai clenched his fists. Veer always had to one-up him, whether it was in exams, sports, or now, science projects. Jai wanted to pick something impressive, something that would make Veer eat his words. But what?

'Hey, Jai,' his friend Rohan called out. 'What are you

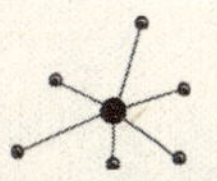

going to do for the assignment?'

Jai sighed. 'I don't know. Everything I think of feels… ordinary. I want to do something no one else is doing.'

Rohan nodded sympathetically. 'Yeah, Veer's already doing Edison, and Ananya's doing Marie Curie. Maybe you should pick something less obvious.'

'Like what?' Jai asked.

Rohan shrugged. 'I don't know. Something about electricity, maybe? That's always cool.'

Electricity. The word sparked something in Jai's mind. He remembered his brother, Nakul, talking about something called an AC motor once. But what was it? And who invented it?

That evening, Jai rushed home and found Nakul tinkering with a broken fan in the garage. 'Nakul, I need your help!' Jai said, panting.

Nakul looked up, wiping grease off his hands. 'What's up, little bro? You look like you've seen a ghost.'

'It's worse than a ghost,' Jai said. 'It's Science Week, and I have no idea what to do for my project. I need something cool, something no one else is doing.'

Nakul grinned. 'Well, you've come to the right person. What about the AC motor? It's one of the most important inventions in history, but most people don't know much about it.'

Jai's eyes lit up. 'That's what I was thinking! But who invented it? And how does it work?'

Nakul pulled up a stool and sat down. 'The AC motor was invented by a guy named Mikhail Dolivo-

Dobrovolsky. He was a Russian engineer who figured out how to use alternating current to power motors. Before that, most motors ran on direct current, which wasn't as efficient.'

Jai leaned forward, fascinated. 'Why is the AC motor so important?'

'Because it changed the world,' Nakul said. 'AC motors are used in everything—fans, washing machines, even trains. They're more efficient and can transmit electricity over long distances. Without Dolivo-Dobrovolsky's invention, we wouldn't have modern electricity as we know it.'

Jai's mind raced with ideas. 'Do you think I could make a model of an AC motor for my assignment?'

Nakul nodded. 'Absolutely. It's a bit complicated, but I can help you. We'll keep it simple so your classmates can understand it.'

Over the next few days, Jai and Nakul worked tirelessly on the project. Nakul explained the science behind the AC motor, while Jai focused on making the model. They used simple materials—copper wire, magnets, and a small battery—to create a basic version of the motor.

'The key is the alternating current,' Nakul explained. 'It changes direction periodically, which makes the motor spin. That's why it's so efficient.'

Jai carefully wound the copper wire around a nail to create the coil. 'So, this coil is like the heart of the motor?'

'Exactly,' Nakul said. 'When the current flows

through it, it creates a magnetic field that interacts with the magnets, making the motor spin.'

By the end of the week, they had a working model. It wasn't perfect, but it spun when connected to the battery, and Jai was thrilled. 'This is so cool! Thank you so much, Nakul.'

Nakul ruffled his hair. 'You did most of the work, little bro. Now, you just have to explain it to your class.'

On the day of the Science Week presentation, Jai stood nervously in front of the class, his model AC motor on the table. Veer had already presented his Edison light bulb, complete with a glowing filament, and the class had been impressed. Jai took a deep breath and began.

'My project is about Mikhail Dolivo-Dobrovolsky and his invention of the first practical AC motor,' Jai said. 'Before his invention, most motors ran on direct current, which wasn't very efficient. Dolivo-Dobrovolsky figured out how to use alternating current to power motors, which changed the world and made all our lives easier.'

He held up the model. 'This is a simple version of an AC motor. When I connect it to the battery, the alternating current makes the coil spin, creating motion. This principle is used in everything from fans to trains.'

Jai demonstrated the motor, and the class watched in awe as it spun to life. Even Veer looked impressed.

'Dolivo-Dobrovolsky's invention made modern electricity possible,' Jai continued. 'Without it, we wouldn't have the technology we rely on today. He may not be as famous as Edison or Tesla, but his work was just as important.'

When Jai finished, the class erupted into applause. Mr Tarun, their science teacher, stood up. 'That was an excellent presentation, Jai. You not only explained the science clearly but also highlighted an inventor who doesn't get enough recognition. Well done!'

Jai felt a surge of pride. He glanced at Veer, who gave him a grudging nod. For once, Jai had come out on top.

After class, Mr Tarun pulled Jai aside. 'I was really impressed by your project, Jai. You put a lot of thought and effort into it. How did you come up with the idea?'

Jai smiled. 'My brother, Nakul, helped me. He's an engineer, and he told me about Dolivo-Dobrovolsky. I thought it was a story worth sharing.'

Mr Tarun nodded. 'Well, you did a fantastic job. Keep up the good work.'

That evening, Jai returned home to find Nakul waiting for him. 'So, how did it go?' Nakul asked.

Jai grinned. 'I won! Mr Tarun said it was the best project in the class.'

Nakul high-fived him. 'I knew you could do it. You're a natural at this stuff.'

Jai felt a warm glow of satisfaction. For the first time, he had beaten Veer at something. But more than that, he had discovered a passion for science and engineering, thanks to his brother and the story of Mikhail Dolivo-Dobrovolsky.

As he sat down for dinner with his family, Jai couldn't stop talking about the project. 'I want to learn more about electricity and motors,' he said. 'Maybe I'll even become an engineer like you, Nakul.'

Nakul smiled. 'You'd make a great engineer, Jai. Just remember, science isn't about winning or beating someone else. It's about curiosity, creativity, and making the world a better place.'

Jai nodded, feeling inspired. He knew there was so much more to learn and discover, and he was ready to take on the challenge.

Archimedes

Discovery: Buoyancy principle; simple machines

Archimedes was an ancient Greek mathematician, scientist, and inventor who lived from around 287 BCE to 212 BCE. Archimedes figured out how levers work and explained the concept of buoyancy—the reason why some things float in water.

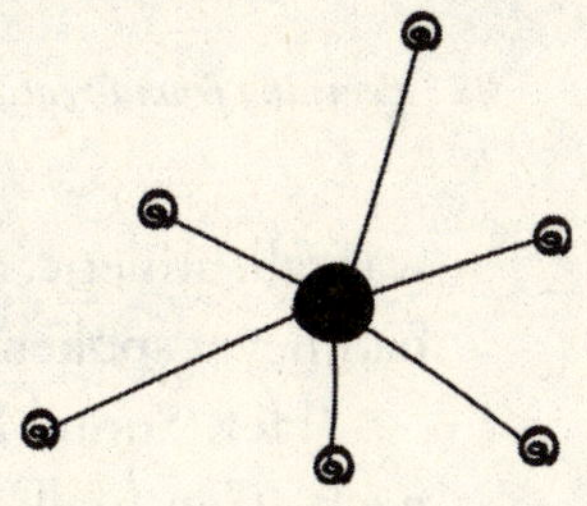

Sonu and the Science Fair

Sonu sat alone at his desk during lunch break, his nose buried in a science textbook. Around him, the classroom buzzed with laughter and chatter as his classmates shared snacks and jokes. But no one invited Sonu to join them. He was used to it by now. Ever since he had started scoring the highest marks in class, everyone had labelled him a 'teacher's pet.' They thought he was too serious, too studious, and too boring to be friends with.

But Sonu didn't mind—or at least, that's what he told himself. He loved learning, and he was proud of his achievements. Still, sometimes he wished someone would talk to him, just once, without rolling their eyes or making a snide comment.

That day, something unexpected happened. As Sonu was packing up his books after school, Himesh, one of the most popular boys in class, approached him. Himesh

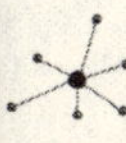

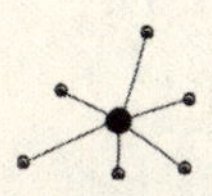

was tall, athletic, and always surrounded by friends. Sonu had never spoken to him before.

'Hey, Sonu,' Himesh said, scratching the back of his neck. 'Can I talk to you for a minute?'

Sonu looked up, surprised. 'Uh, sure. What's up?'

Himesh hesitated. 'So, you know the Science Fair is coming up, right? Well, I'm supposed to do a project, but… I have no idea what to do. I was wondering if you could help me.'

Sonu blinked. 'You want my help?'

'Yeah,' Himesh said. 'I mean, you're the smartest kid in class. You always know the answers. I thought maybe you could give me some ideas.'

Sonu felt a warm glow in his chest. No one had ever asked for his help before. 'Of course, I'll help you! What kind of project are you thinking of?'

Himesh shrugged. 'I don't know. Something cool, I guess. But not too complicated.'

Sonu thought for a moment. Then his face lit up. 'What about Archimedes' principle? It's really interesting, and we can make a fun experiment to demonstrate it.'

Himesh frowned. 'Archimedes' what?'

'Archimedes' principle,' Sonu repeated. 'It's about buoyancy—why things float or sink. Archimedes was this ancient Greek mathematician and scientist who lived over 2,000 years ago. He's famous for discovering this principle, and there's a cool story behind it.'

Himesh raised an eyebrow. 'A story? Like, a real story?'

'Yeah,' Sonu said, grinning. 'Archimedes was trying

to figure out if a gold crown made for the king was pure gold or if it had been mixed with cheaper metals. He was stuck on the problem until one day, while taking a bath, he noticed how the water level rose when he got into the tub. That's when it hit him—he could use water displacement to measure the crown's volume and figure out if it was real gold. He was so excited that he ran through the streets naked, shouting 'Eureka!' which means 'I found it!' in Greek.'

Himesh burst out laughing. 'That's hilarious! Okay, I'm in. Tell me more.'

Over the next few days, Sonu and Himesh worked together on the project. Sonu explained the science behind Archimedes' principle, while Himesh helped with the hands-on part. They decided to create a simple experiment using a tub of water, a small boat, and some weights.

'The principle states that the buoyant force on an object is equal to the weight of the fluid it displaces,' Sonu explained as they set up the experiment. 'So, if the boat displaces enough water, it will float. But if we add too much weight, it will sink.'

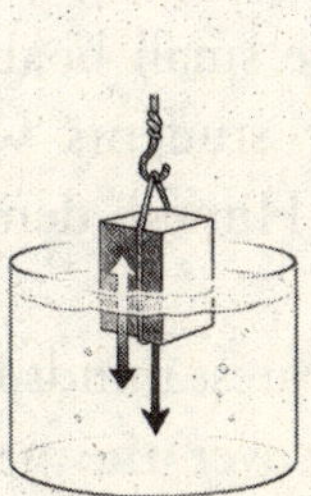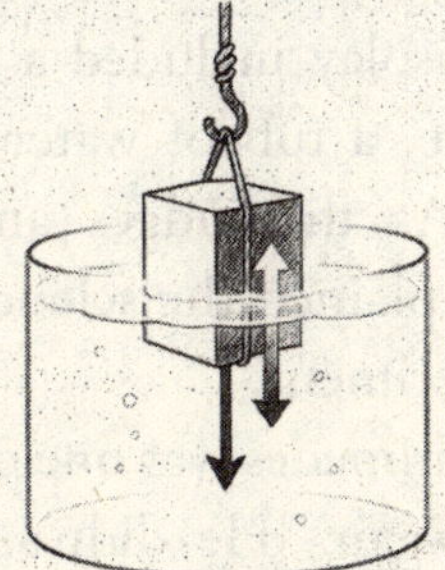

Himesh nodded, though he still looked a little confused. 'Okay, but how do we show that?'

'We'll measure the water level before and after adding weights,' Sonu said. 'That way, we can prove that the boat displaces more water as it gets heavier.'

Himesh grinned. 'That sounds cool. Let's do it.'

As they worked, Sonu couldn't help but feel happy. For the first time, someone was treating him like a friend, not just the class nerd. Himesh even laughed at his jokes and asked him questions about other science topics.

'You know, Sonu,' Himesh said one afternoon, 'you're not as boring as everyone says you are.'

Sonu blinked. 'Uh… thanks?'

Himesh laughed. 'I mean, you're actually pretty fun to hang out with. I don't know why no one talks to you.'

Sonu shrugged. 'I guess they think I'm too serious or something.'

'Well, they're wrong,' Himesh said. 'You're cool. And after this project, I'm going to make sure everyone knows it.'

On the day of the science fair, Sonu and Himesh set up their experiment at a table in the school auditorium. Their display included a poster explaining Archimedes' principle, a tub of water, and the small boat they had made. As the judges and other students walked by, Sonu explained the science while Himesh demonstrated the experiment.

'Archimedes was one of the greatest minds in history,' Sonu began. 'He didn't just discover the principle of buoyancy—he also invented things like the Archimedes screw, which is still used today to move water. He was a genius who combined math and science to solve real-world problems.'

Himesh added, 'And he did it all over 2,000 years ago, without any of the tools we have today. Pretty impressive, right?'

The audience nodded, clearly fascinated. Sonu continued, 'When we add weights to the boat, it sinks lower into the water. This is because the boat has to displace more water to stay afloat. If we add too much weight, the boat will sink completely.'

Himesh added a few weights to the boat, and the audience watched as it slowly sank. 'See? The boat can only handle so much weight before it can't displace enough water to stay afloat.'

The judges were impressed. 'This is a great demonstration of Archimedes' principle,' one of them said. 'You've explained it clearly and made it easy to understand. Well done!'

After the fair, their Science teacher, Mrs Sharma, called them over. 'I have to say, I'm very proud of both of you. This was an excellent project, and you worked well together.'

Himesh grinned. 'Thanks, ma'am. But it was mostly Sonu's idea. He's the real genius here.'

Sonu blushed. 'It was a team effort. Himesh did a lot of the work too.'

Mrs Sharma smiled. 'Well, you make a great team. Keep up the good work.'

As they packed up their project, Himesh turned to Sonu. 'Hey, I was thinking… maybe we could hang out sometime. You know, outside of school.'

Sonu's eyes widened. 'Really? You mean it?'

'Of course,' Himesh said. 'You're a cool guy, Sonu. I don't know why I didn't see it before. And I promise, I'll introduce you to my friends. They'll like you too.'

Sonu felt a lump in his throat. For the first time in a long while, he felt like he belonged. 'Thanks, Himesh. That means a lot.'

Himesh slung an arm around his shoulder. 'No problem. That's what friends are for, right?'

As they walked out of the auditorium together, Sonu couldn't stop smiling. He had always been the smartest kid in class, but now, for the first time, he felt like he had something even more important—a friend.

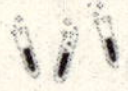

Charles Goodyear

Invention: Vulcanized rubber

Charles Goodyear was an American inventor who lived from 1800 to 1860. He is best known for discovering the process of Vulcanization, which makes rubber strong, flexible, and able to withstand heat and cold.

This discovery changed his life and the future of rubber manufacturing. Although he didn't become rich from his invention, Goodyear's work had a huge impact on industry and transportation.

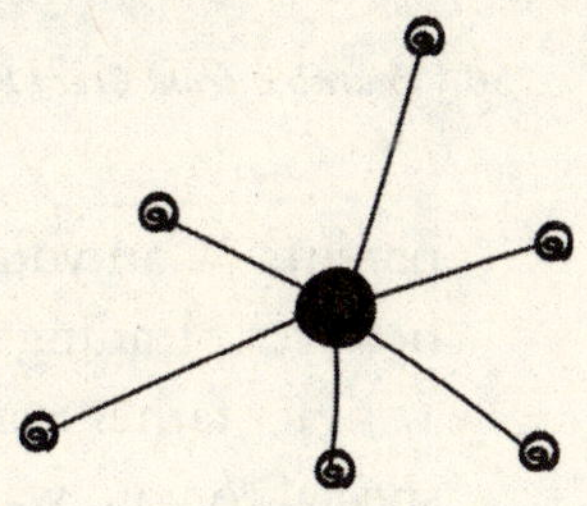

Noorie and the Bouncy Ball

Noorie sat on the edge of the playground, staring at the broken pieces of her favorite bouncy ball. It had been a bright red ball, the kind that bounced higher than any other ball she had ever owned. She had been playing with her friends, Riya and Aanya, when it had hit a sharp rock and split into two. Noorie's heart sank as she picked up the pieces. She loved that ball—it had been a gift from her parents on her last birthday.

'Noorie, don't be sad,' Riya said, patting her shoulder. 'It's just a ball. You can get another one.'

'Yeah,' Aanya added. 'Your parents will buy you a new one.'

But Noorie wasn't so sure. Her parents had always encouraged her to take care of her things. 'What if they say no?' she wondered aloud.

That evening, Noorie showed the broken ball to her

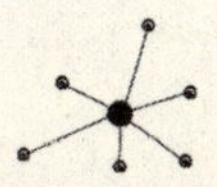

parents. 'Can you buy me a new one, please?' she asked, her eyes pleading.

Her father examined the pieces. 'Noorie, this ball was special to you, wasn't it?'

Noorie nodded. 'It was my favourite.'

Her mother sat down beside her. 'We can buy you a new ball, but first, I want you to learn something. Do you know how this ball was made?'

Noorie frowned. 'No. It's just rubber, right?'

'Yes, but rubber doesn't just grow on trees—well, actually, it does, but it's not that simple,' her mother said with a smile. 'Why don't you find out how rubber is made and turned into things like bouncy balls? Then we'll talk about getting you a new one.'

Noorie sighed. She didn't want to do homework about rubber; she just wanted a new ball. But she knew her parents wouldn't budge. 'Okay,' she said reluctantly. 'I'll find out.'

The next day, Noorie decided to visit her grandma, who was a retired college professor. Grandma always had interesting stories and answers to Noorie's questions. She lived in a cosy house filled with books and plants, and Noorie loved spending time with her.

'Grandma,' Noorie said as soon as she arrived, 'do you know how bouncy balls are made?'

Grandma smiled. 'Ah, that's a great question. It all starts with rubber. Do you know where rubber comes from?'

'From trees?' Noorie guessed.

'Exactly,' Grandma said. 'Rubber comes from the sap of rubber trees. But raw rubber isn't very useful—it's sticky and can melt in the heat. That's where Charles Goodyear comes in.'

'Who's Charles Goodyear?' Noorie asked, intrigued.

'He was an inventor who discovered a process called Vulcanization,' Grandma explained. 'Back in the 1800s, people were trying to find a way to make rubber stronger and more durable. Charles Goodyear spent years experimenting, and one day, he accidentally dropped a mixture of rubber and sulfur onto a hot stove. Instead of melting, the rubber became stronger and more elastic. That's how vulcanization was discovered.'

Noorie's eyes widened. 'So, he made rubber better by accident?'

'Yes,' Grandma said with a laugh. 'Sometimes, the best discoveries happen by chance. Vulcanization changed the world. It made rubber useful for all sorts of things—tyres, shoes, and yes, even bouncy balls.'

Noorie thought for a moment. 'Can we see a rubber tree? I want to know how it all starts.'

Grandma's eyes twinkled. 'I was hoping you'd ask. There's a botanical garden nearby that has rubber trees. Let's go there and see for ourselves.'

The botanical garden was a lush, green paradise filled with plants from all over the world. Grandma led Noorie to a section where tall rubber trees grew. The trees had smooth bark, and some of them had small cuts with white sap dripping into containers below.

'This is latex,' Grandma said, pointing to the sap. 'It's collected and processed to make raw rubber.'

Noorie watched as a gardener demonstrated how the sap was collected. 'It looks like milk,' she said.

'Yes, but it's stickier,' Grandma said. 'Once the latex is collected, it's treated with chemicals to make it solid. Then it's rolled into sheets and dried.'

'And that's how rubber is made?' Noorie asked.

'Not quite,' Grandma said. 'Raw rubber still needs to be vulcanized to make it strong and elastic. That's where Charles Goodyear's discovery comes in.'

Noorie nodded, her curiosity growing. 'Can we see how vulcanization works?'

Grandma smiled. 'We can't do it here, but I can show you a simple experiment at home to explain the process.'

Back at Grandma's house, they set up a small experiment. Grandma took a piece of raw rubber and heated it with sulfur. 'This is a simplified version of Vulcanization,' she said. 'When the rubber is heated with sulfur, it forms cross-links between the rubber molecules, making it stronger and more elastic.'

Noorie watched as the rubber changed texture. 'It's like magic!' she exclaimed.

'Science is often like magic,' Grandma said with a wink. 'But it's magic we can understand and use.'

Noorie thought about her bouncy ball. 'So, my ball was made from rubber that went through this process?'

'Exactly,' Grandma said. 'The rubber was vulcanized, then shaped and coloured to make your bouncy ball.'

Noorie felt a sense of wonder. She had never thought about how much work went into making something as simple as a bouncy ball. 'I think I understand now,' she said. 'Rubber comes from trees, and it's made stronger through vulcanization. That's how my ball was made.'

Grandma nodded. 'And now that you know, you can appreciate it even more.'

When Noorie returned home, she told her parents everything she had learned. 'Rubber comes from trees, and Charles Goodyear made it stronger with vulcanization. That's how my bouncy ball was made.'

Her parents smiled. 'We're proud of you, Noorie,' her father said. 'You worked hard to learn something new.'

'Does that mean I can get a new ball now?' Noorie asked hopefully.

Her mother laughed. 'Yes, you can. But remember, take good care of it. And maybe one day, you'll make a discovery as important as Charles Goodyear's.'

Noorie grinned. 'Maybe I will.'

The next day, Noorie went to the store with her parents and picked out a new bouncy ball—this time, a bright blue one. As she bounced it on the sidewalk, she thought about rubber trees, Vulcanization, and the thrilling journey that had turned sap into something so fun.

'Noorie, come play!' Riya called from the playground.

Noorie ran to join her friends, her new ball in hand. She felt proud of what she had learned and happy to have her favorite toy back. But more than that, she felt a new sense of curiosity about the world and how things worked.

As she played, she couldn't help but smile. Science wasn't just something she read about in books—it was all around her, even in something as simple as a bouncy ball.

Samuel Morse

Invention: Morse code; telegraph

Samuel Morse was an American inventor and artist who lived from 1791 to 1872. He is best known for inventing the telegraph and co-developing Morse code, a system of dots and dashes used to send messages over long distances. Before the telegraph, it could take days or even weeks for news to travel. Morse's invention made it possible to communicate across great distances in just minutes, which changed the world forever.

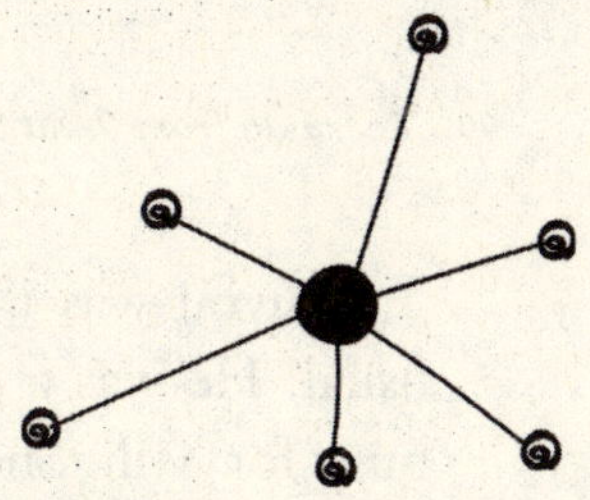

Mili and the Telegraph Key

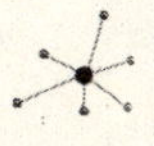

Mili stood in the middle of her grandfather's dusty attic, staring at the pile of old belongings she had been tasked with cleaning. Her parents had given her the job as part of their annual spring cleaning ritual, and while Mili didn't mind the work, she wasn't exactly thrilled about it either. The attic was filled with boxes, old furniture, and mysterious objects that seemed to belong to another era.

As she sorted through a box of her grandfather's things, something caught her eye—a small, brass device with a lever and a knob. It looked like a strange toy, but Mili had no idea what it was. She turned it over in her hands, trying to make sense of it. There were wires attached to it, and the words 'Telegraph Key' were engraved on the side.

'What is this thing?' Mili muttered to herself. She pressed the lever, and it made a clicking sound. Intrigued, she decided to ask her older brother, Yuvraj, for help.

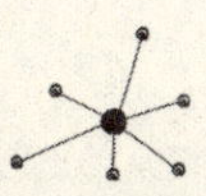

Yuvraj was in his room, glued to his computer, as usual. He was a college student and always seemed too busy for Mili. She knocked on his door and held up the brass device. 'Yuvraj, do you know what this is?'

He glanced at it briefly. 'Oh, that's a telegraph key. It's used for Morse code.'

'Morse code?' Mili asked, her curiosity piqued.

'Yeah, it's a way to send messages using dots and dashes,' Yuvraj said, already turning back to his computer. 'Look it up if you're interested. I've got work to do.'

Mili frowned. Yuvraj was always like this—too busy to explain anything properly. But his brief explanation had sparked her interest. She decided to do some research on her own.

That evening, Mili sat at her desk with her laptop, typing 'Morse code' into the search bar. She quickly learned that Morse code was a system of communication invented by Samuel Morse in the 1830s. It used a series of dots and dashes to represent letters and numbers, which could be sent over long distances using a telegraph.

'Samuel Morse was an artist and inventor,' Mili read aloud. 'He created the Telegraph and Morse code to make communication faster and more efficient.'

She scrolled through images of old telegraph machines and diagrams of Morse code. The idea of sending secret messages using dots and dashes fascinated her. She wondered if she could use the telegraph key she had found to send messages like they did in the old days.

The next day, Mili told her friends, Jhilmil and

Piyushi, about her discovery. 'We should make our own telegraph system!' she said excitedly. 'We can send secret messages to each other.'

Jhilmil, who loved puzzles and codes, was immediately on board. 'That sounds so cool! But how do we make a telegraph?'

'I'm not sure,' Mili admitted. 'But we can figure it out together.'

Piyushi, the practical one of the group, suggested they start by learning Morse code. 'If we're going to send messages, we need to know how to write and read them.'

The three friends spent the next few days practicing Morse code. They made flashcards with the dots and dashes for each letter and quizzed each other. Mili even found an old book in the library that explained how telegraph systems worked.

'We need wires, a battery, and something to make sound,' Mili said, reading from the book. 'The telegraph key is just the switch that opens and closes the circuit.'

Jhilmil's eyes lit up. 'My dad has a toolbox with wires and batteries. I'll ask him if we can use some.'

Piyushi nodded. 'And we can use a buzzer or a light bulb to make the signals.'

With Jhilmil's supplies and Piyushi's technical skills, the girls built a simple telegraph system. They connected the telegraph key to a battery and a small buzzer, creating a circuit that would make a sound every time the key was pressed.

'It works!' Mili exclaimed as she pressed the key and the buzzer clicked. 'Now we just need to set it up between our houses.'

The girls decided to set up their telegraph system between Mili's house and Jhilmil's house, which were across the street from each other. They ran a long wire between the two houses, careful to keep it hidden so no one would trip over it. They set up the telegraph key and buzzer at each end, creating a simple but functional communication system.

'Okay, let's try it,' Mili said, sitting at her end of the telegraph. She pressed the key in a pattern of dots and dashes, sending the message 'HI' to Jhilmil.

At the other end, Jhilmil listened to the buzzer and wrote down the dots and dashes. 'It says 'HI'!' she called back.

The girls cheered. Their telegraph system worked! Over the next few days, they sent messages back and forth, practicing their Morse code skills and coming up with secret codes for fun.

One afternoon, Mili had an idea. 'Let's send a message to my grandma. She lives just down the street, and I think she'd love to see what we've made.'

The girls ran a wire to Mili's grandmother's house and set up a buzzer there. Mili's grandmother, who had been a science teacher before retiring, was delighted by the project. 'This reminds me of the old days,' she said with a smile. 'Your grandfather used to love tinkering with things like this.'

Mili's heart warmed at the mention of her grandfather. 'We want to send you a message,' she said. 'It's a thank-you note.'

The girls worked together to send the message in Morse code: 'THANK YOU FOR INSPIRING US.'

Mili's grandmother listened carefully to the buzzer and decoded the message. When she realised what it said, her eyes filled with tears. 'Oh, girls, this is wonderful. Your grandfather would have been so proud of you.'

Mili felt a lump in her throat. She had never known her grandfather well—he had passed away when she was very young—but she felt a connection to him through the telegraph key and the stories her grandmother told.

That evening, Mili sat with her grandmother, looking through old photos of her grandfather. 'He was a scientist, just like you,' her grandmother said. 'He loved inventing things and solving problems. This telegraph key was one of his favourite tools.'

Mili smiled. 'I'm glad I found it. It made me learn

something new, and it brought me closer to him.'

Her grandmother hugged her. 'He would have loved to see what you and your friends created. You're carrying on his legacy.'

As Mili went to bed that night, she felt a sense of pride and gratitude. She had started the day with a simple task—cleaning the attic—but it had turned into an adventure that taught her about history, science, and her own family.

The next morning, she found Yuvraj in the kitchen and told him everything she had learned. 'Thanks for telling me about Morse code,' she said. 'It led to something really special.'

Yuvraj smiled, a rare moment of warmth from her usually busy brother. 'I'm glad you figured it out, Mili. You're pretty smart, you know.'

Mili grinned. 'I know.'

As she left the kitchen, she thought about the telegraph key and the messages it had sent. It wasn't just a tool for communication—it was a bridge between the past and the present, connecting her to her grandfather and to a world of discovery.

And she couldn't wait to see what she would learn next.

Michael Faraday

Invention: Electromagnetic induction

Michael Faraday was a British scientist who lived from 1791 to 1867. He made major discoveries in the fields of electricity and magnetism, and his work helped shape the modern world.

Faraday discovered electromagnetic induction, which is how electricity can be generated by moving a magnet near a coil of wire. This discovery led to the creation of electric generators and motors, which power many of the machines we use today.

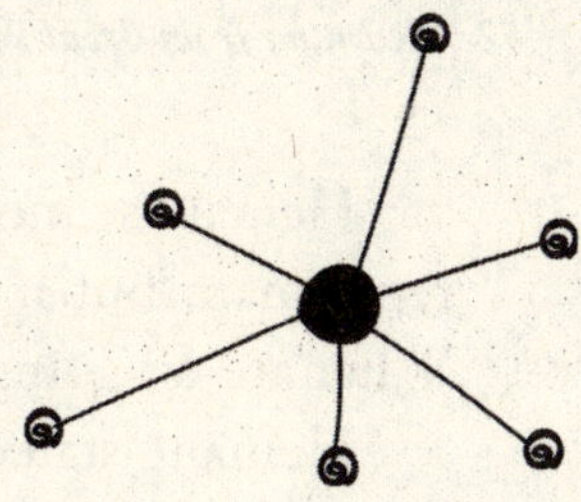

Hemant and the Broken Refrigerator

The heatwave had arrived without warning, turning Hemant's small town into an oven. The sun blazed relentlessly, and the air felt thick and heavy. Hemant's family had been relying on their refrigerator to keep their food fresh and their drinks cold, but on the third day of the heatwave, disaster struck.

'Hemant, come here!' his mother called from the kitchen. Her voice was tense, and Hemant knew something was wrong.

He rushed to the kitchen to find his parents standing in front of the refrigerator, which was ominously silent. The usual hum of the motor was gone, and the inside was already starting to feel warm.

'It's broken,' his father said, running a hand through his hair. 'And with this heatwave, we can't afford to lose our food.'

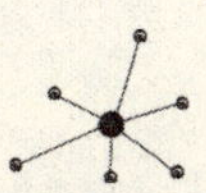

Hemant's mother sighed. 'We'll have to call a repairman, but it might take hours for them to come. What are we going to do until then?'

Hemant stared at the lifeless refrigerator, feeling a mix of frustration and curiosity. 'How does a refrigerator even work?' he wondered aloud.

His father glanced at him. 'It's all about cooling and heat transfer. But I don't know the details.'

Hemant's curiosity was piqued. 'Maybe I can figure it out. If I understand how it works, maybe I can help fix it—or at least find a way to keep our food cold until the repairman comes.'

His father raised an eyebrow. 'That's a big task, Hemant. But if you're serious, I'll help you.'

Hemant spent the rest of the day researching refrigeration. He learned that the modern refrigerator was based on principles discovered by scientists like Michael Faraday, who had experimented with the liquefaction of gases and the absorption of heat. Faraday's work had laid the foundation for the refrigeration cycle, which involved compressing and expanding gases to remove heat from an enclosed space.

'So, it's all about moving heat from inside the refrigerator to the outside,' Hemant said, summarising what he had read. 'But without electricity, we can't run the compressor.'

His father nodded. 'That's right. But there are other ways to cool things down. People have been keeping food cold for centuries, even before refrigerators were invented.'

Hemant's eyes lit up. 'Like evaporative cooling? I read about that. It's how clay pots keep water cool.'

'Exactly,' his father said. 'Evaporative cooling uses water to absorb heat. Maybe we can build something simple to keep our food from spoiling.'

The next morning, Hemant and his father gathered materials to build an evaporative cooler. They used a large cardboard box, a shallow tray, a small fan, and some cloth. Hemant's mother donated an old bedsheet, which they cut into strips.

'The idea is to create a flow of air over water,' Hemant explained as they worked. 'When the water evaporates, it absorbs heat, cooling the air inside the box.'

His father helped him set up the tray at the bottom of the box and filled it with water. They hung the cloth strips so that one end was in the water and the other end was exposed to the air. The fan was placed at one end of the box to draw air through the wet cloth.

'Let's test it,' Hemant said, plugging in the fan.

The fan whirred to life, pulling air through the damp cloth. Hemant placed a thermometer inside the box and waited. After a few minutes, he checked the temperature.

'It's working!' he exclaimed. 'The temperature inside the box is dropping.'

His father smiled. 'Good job, Hemant. Now let's see if it can keep our food cool.'

They moved the evaporative cooler to the pantry and placed their perishable food inside. It wasn't as cold as a refrigerator, but it was enough to prevent spoilage until the repairman arrived.

Over the next few days, Hemant continued to learn about refrigeration and cooling. He read about Michael Faraday's experiments with ammonia and how early refrigerators used toxic gases before safer alternatives were developed. He also learned about the environmental impact of modern refrigerants and the importance of energy efficiency.

'It's amazing how much science goes into something we take for granted,' Hemant said to his father one evening. 'I never thought about how a refrigerator works until ours broke.'

His father nodded. 'Sometimes, it takes a problem to make us appreciate the things we have. And you've done a great job finding a solution.'

Hemant smiled. 'Thanks, Dad. I couldn't have done it without your help.'

When the repairman finally arrived, he was impressed

by their makeshift cooler. 'That's a clever solution,' he said. 'You've got the basics of evaporative cooling down pat.'

Hemant felt a surge of pride. 'I learned a lot about refrigeration while we were waiting for you. It's fascinating how it all works.'

The repairman chuckled. 'Well, you've got a bright future ahead of you if you're already tinkering with things like this.'

As the refrigerator hummed back to life, Hemant felt a sense of accomplishment. He had not only helped his family through a difficult time but also gained a deeper understanding of the science behind everyday technology.

That night, as he lay in bed, Hemant thought about Michael Faraday and the other scientists who had paved the way for modern refrigeration. Their curiosity and ingenuity had changed the world, and Hemant felt inspired to follow in their footsteps.

'Maybe I'll be a scientist one day,' he thought. 'Or an engineer. There's so much to discover and invent.'

With the heatwave finally breaking and the refrigerator back in working order, Hemant drifted off to sleep, dreaming of cool breeze and endless possibilities.

Rachel Carson

Environmental impact of pesticides

Rachel Carson was an American marine biologist, writer, and environmentalist who lived from 1907 to 1964. She is best known for her book *Silent Spring*, published in 1962, which warned people about the harmful effects of pesticides on the environment. Her writing showed how chemicals like DDT were damaging birds, animals, and even humans. The book raised public awareness and led to stronger environmental protections and the eventual ban of DDT in many countries.

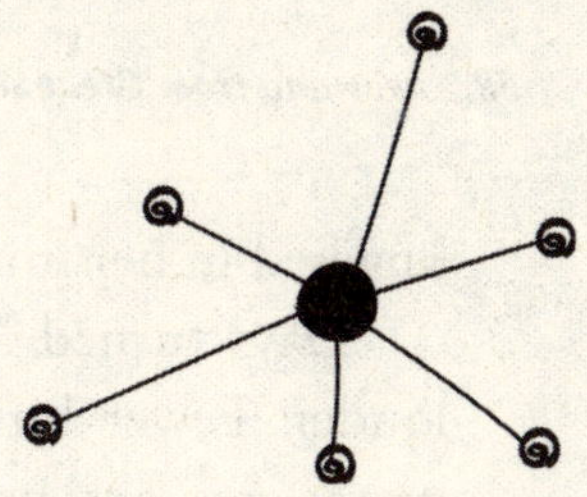

Saumya and the Song of the Birds

Twelve-year-old Saumya Kapoor loved her small corner of the world. The rustling leaves of the oak trees, the bright splashes of colour from the wildflowers, and most of all—the birds. Every afternoon after school, Saumya could be found sitting on a wooden bench in Maple Grove Park, her sketchbook open on her lap. She had learned the names of almost every bird that visited the park, from the vibrant cardinals to the cheerful robins that hopped through the grass.

But something was different lately.

Saumya first noticed it on a warm afternoon in early spring. She had been sketching a blue jay perched on a branch when she realised how quiet it was. No chorus of chirps, no fluttering wings. The usual symphony of bird calls had become... muted.

Maybe I'm imagining it, she thought, but the feeling

lingered in her mind like an unanswered question.

Days turned into weeks, and the silence only grew louder. Fewer birds visited the feeders near the park's picnic area, and her sketches, once filled with lively birds, now captured only empty branches.

'Where did they go?'

That question echoed in Saumya's mind.

One afternoon, she decided to talk to Mr Patel, the friendly groundskeeper who had tended to the park for as long as she could remember. His weathered hands were pulling weeds from the flower beds when she approached.

'Mr Patel, have you noticed fewer birds around lately?' Saumya asked, her voice filled with concern.

Mr Patel wiped his forehead and nodded slowly.

'I have,' he said. 'Used to be, the park was alive with songbirds this time of year. But lately... it's been too quiet.'

Saumya frowned. 'Do you know why?'

Mr Patel glanced around the park and sighed. 'Could be a lot of things. Habitat changes, weather... but sometimes, it's what we don't see that causes the most harm.'

Saumya's brow furrowed. What did that mean?

That evening, Saumya sat at her desk, her notebook open and her laptop humming softly. She was determined to find out what was happening to the birds.

As she typed, she stumbled across the name *Rachel Carson*—a scientist and writer who had changed the world by uncovering the dangers of pesticides in her groundbreaking book, *Silent Spring*.

Saumya's eyes widened as she read about how chemicals sprayed on crops had seeped into the environment, poisoning insects and disrupting the delicate balance of nature. Birds that fed on those insects became sick, and entire ecosystems were thrown off balance.

Could something like that be happening here?

The next day, Saumya visited the library after school. She borrowed *Silent Spring* and read it cover to cover over the weekend. Carson's words echoed in her mind:

'We stand now where two roads diverge… The road we have long been traveling is deceptively easy—a smooth superhighway on which we progress with great speed, but at its end lies disaster.'

Saumya's heart pounded. She needed to do something.

Determined to uncover the truth, Saumya began her own investigation. She started by talking to people who might know more.

She spoke to Mrs Gonzalez, who lived near the park and had a beautiful garden filled with native plants.

'The bees haven't been visiting as much either,' Mrs Gonzalez said with a worried frown. 'It's strange. Something's not right.'

Saumya also interviewed Mr Patel again, asking about any recent changes in the park.

'Well,' he said thoughtfully, 'the city's been spraying for mosquitoes lately. A new pesticide, I think. They say it's safe, but… who really knows?'

Pesticides.

Saumya's heart sank. Could this be the cause?

Saumya knew she couldn't rely on guesses. She needed evidence.

Using her savings, she bought a water testing kit and collected samples from the park's pond and nearby soil. Her science teacher, Mr Harris, helped her analyse the results after school.

As they peered at the data, Mr Harris frowned.

'High traces of chemicals,' he muttered. 'Definitely pesticides.'

Saumya's stomach twisted.

'This could be what's harming the birds,' she whispered.

Mr Harris nodded solemnly. 'It's possible. But proving it—and convincing people to take action— won't be easy.'

Saumya clenched her fists. 'Then I'll make them listen.'

Saumya knew she needed help. She couldn't save the birds alone.

She spent the next week creating flyers and a website called *Save Our Songbirds*. She included everything she had learned about pesticides and their effects on wildlife. Her goal? To rally the community to protect the park and its inhabitants.

During lunch breaks, she convinced her friends to help spread the word. They passed out flyers at school, spoke to neighbour, and even convinced the local community centre to let them hold a *Save Our Songbirds* meeting.

On the day of the meeting, Saumya stood at the front of the community centre, her heart pounding as people filled the room. Parents, teachers, bird watchers, and even local officials gathered, curious to hear what she had to say.

Taking a deep breath, Saumya began.

'I've been coming to Maple Grove Park since I was little,' she said, her voice steady despite her nerves. 'I've watched the birds here every day. But now... they're disappearing.'

She spoke about her investigation, the evidence she had found, and the harmful effects of pesticides. She quoted Rachel Carson, explaining how small changes in the environment could lead to devastating consequences.

'We need to create a safe place for the birds,' Saumya concluded, her eyes scanning the room. 'But I can't do it alone. Will you help me?'

For a moment, silence filled the room. Then, one by one, hands began to rise.

With the community's support, Saumya's project took flight.

The first step was convincing the city council to stop using harmful pesticides in the park. Saumya and her friends gathered petitions and presented their case at a council meeting. Thanks to their research and the voices of the community, the council agreed to explore safer, eco-friendly alternatives.

Next, Saumya organised a community planting event. Inspired by Rachel Carson's love of native plants,

she worked with Mrs Gonzalez to select flowers and shrubs that would attract pollinators and provide food and shelter for the birds.

Families came with shovels and gloves, transforming the park into a thriving habitat. They built birdhouses, placed feeders filled with seeds, and planted milkweed to welcome butterflies.

As weeks passed, the change was visible. Bees buzzed around the flowers, and the air slowly filled with the sweet sound of chirping birds once more.

One sunny afternoon, Saumya sat on her favourite bench in Maple Grove Park, her sketchbook open. But this time, she wasn't sketching empty branches.

A pair of bluebirds flitted near a newly built birdhouse, and a cardinal called from a nearby tree. The symphony of nature had returned.

Mr Patel walked by and smiled at her. 'You did good,

Saumya,' he said, his voice filled with pride.

Saumya beamed.

'It wasn't just me,' she replied softly. 'It was all of us.'

As she watched the birds flit and sing, Saumya thought about Rachel Carson and her words—how one voice could inspire change, how even the smallest actions could ripple outward and make a difference.

The park was alive again, and so was Saumya's hope for the future.

This is just the beginning, she thought with a smile.

Because when people listened to nature's song, they could always find a way to keep it alive.

And Saumya?

She was ready to listen, protect, and keep the song going.

Thomas Edison

Invention: Practical electric light bulb; phonograph

Thomas Edison was an American inventor and businessman who lived from 1847 to 1931. He is best known for inventing the practical electric light bulb, which changed the way people lived and worked. He also created many other useful inventions, including the phonograph (an early music player) and the motion picture camera. His work helped shape the modern world and earned him the nickname 'The Wizard of Menlo Park'.

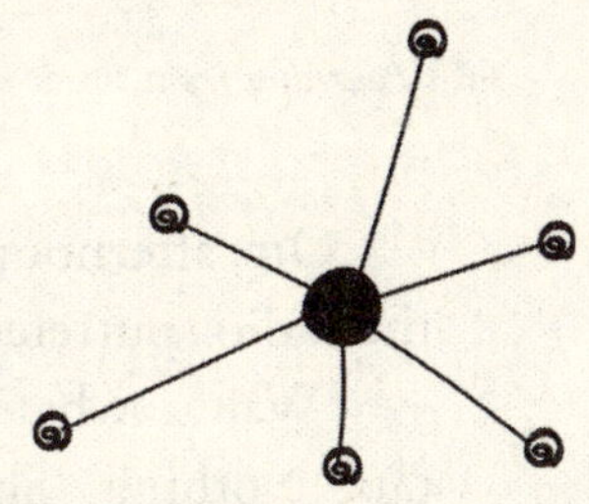

Samridhi and the Sound
of Discovery

Twelve-year-old Samridhi Sharma couldn't imagine a day without music. Whether it was the upbeat Bollywood hits her mother played while cooking or the old classics her grandfather hummed while sitting on the porch, music was woven into the fabric of her life.

But Samridhi's favourite way to enjoy music was through her trusty little radio. It was an old, slightly worn-out model that her father had given her on her tenth birthday. Every evening after finishing her homework, Samridhi would curl up on her bed, tune into her favourite station, and let the melodies carry her away.

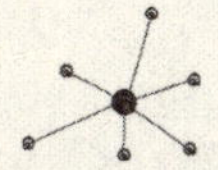

One afternoon, just as her favourite song was playing, the radio sputtered and went silent.

'Wait... what?' Samridhi frowned, giving it a light tap. Nothing. She adjusted the antenna, twisted the knobs, and even tried shaking it gently—still, no sound.

Her heart sank.

Samridhi carried the silent radio to the living room where her parents were sipping tea and reading.

'Papa, my radio stopped working!' she said, holding it up as if displaying an injured friend.

Her father looked up, setting his newspaper aside.

'Hmm... it's pretty old, *beta,*' he said. 'Maybe it's time to get a new one.'

Samridhi's eyes brightened. 'Really? Can we buy one today?'

Her mother, however, smiled gently and exchanged a glance with her father.

'Not so fast,' her mother said, her eyes twinkling with mischief. 'How about we make a deal?'

Samridhi tilted her head, curious.

'We'll get you a new radio,' her father said, 'but only after you learn about the history of communication— how sound was first recorded and shared.'

Samridhi blinked. 'The... history of communication?'

Her father nodded, leaning back in his chair. 'If you want to appreciate how far we've come, it's important to know where it all started.'

Samridhi sighed, but curiosity sparked in her mind. She loved learning new things, and if it would get her a new radio... why not?

'Okay,' she agreed, determination gleaming in her eyes. 'Challenge accepted.'

The very next day, Samridhi rode her bicycle to the local library. It was a cosy, two-story building that smelled of old books and fresh paper. She loved how the sunlight streamed through the large windows, making the wooden shelves glow softly.

'History of communication... history of communication...' she mumbled, scanning the shelves.

After a few minutes, she found a book titled *The Story of Sound: From Phonographs to Podcasts*. She eagerly flipped through the pages, and that's when she discovered Thomas Edison.

Her eyes widened as she read about the phonograph—a device Edison had invented in 1877.

'Edison's phonograph could record sound on a tinfoil-covered cylinder,' Samridhi murmured. 'And when the cylinder was played back, it repeated the recorded sound!'

Her imagination soared. Imagine how amazed people must have been to hear their own voices played back for the first time!

Samridhi spent hours reading about early sound recording devices—the phonograph, the gramophone, and even magnetic tape recorders. She learned how sound waves could be captured, stored, and reproduced using vibrations and grooves.

As she closed the book, an idea began to take shape in her mind.

When Samridhi returned home that evening, her mind was buzzing with possibilities. She had learned about the evolution of sound recording, but instead of asking her parents for a new radio, a new idea had taken root.

She rushed to her room, grabbed her notebook, and began sketching ideas.

'I can't make a real phonograph,' she murmured, tapping her pencil against her chin, 'but maybe I can build something simple... something that records and plays back sound.'

Her eyes darted around the room, scanning for materials.

Over the next few days, Samridhi gathered supplies. She rummaged through drawers and shelves, collecting bits and pieces:

- An old plastic cup
- A sewing needle from her mother's kit
- A balloon for creating a diaphragm
- A few rubber bands
- A spool of thread

Her father watched as she worked at the dining table, his curiosity growing.

'What are you up to, beta?' he finally asked one evening.

Samridhi grinned but kept her project a secret. 'You'll see,' she said with a wink.

Samridhi followed the principles she had learned about the phonograph. She stretched the balloon tightly over the top of the plastic cup, securing it with rubber bands. Then, she carefully attached the sewing needle to the centre of the balloon.

To her amazement, the contraption was starting to look a little like the simple sound recorders she had read about.

Next, she wound the thread around the spool and pressed the needle gently against it.

'Okay,' she whispered, her heart pounding with excitement.

She spoke softly into the balloon's surface, her voice vibrating the stretched material and moving the needle. As the thread spun, the needle etched faint grooves into it.

Now came the tricky part—playing it back.

Samridhi carefully reversed the motion, dragging the needle back over the grooves she had created. She leaned in close, holding her breath.

At first, there was only a faint scratching sound.

Come on...

And then.

'Hello...'

The sound was faint, scratchy, and distorted... but it was there. Her own voice, coming back to her from the grooves she had created.

Her eyes widened, and a huge grin spread across her face.

'I did it!'

Samridhi couldn't wait to show her parents. She carefully brought her homemade sound recorder to the living room, where her parents were reading.

'Papa, Ma,' she said, her voice brimming with excitement, 'I have something to show you.'

Her parents exchanged curious glances as Samridhi demonstrated her creation. She spoke softly into the makeshift microphone, spun the thread, and then played it back.

'Hello...'

Her father's eyebrows shot up. 'Samridhi! Did you... did you build this yourself?'

Samridhi nodded, her eyes shining with pride.

'I learned about the phonograph and how sound is recorded,' she explained eagerly. 'And I thought... instead of asking for a new radio, I'd try to make something that could record sound myself!'

Her mother's eyes misted with pride, and her father's face lit up with admiration.

'This is incredible, beta,' her father said softly. 'You didn't just learn about the history of communication... you brought it to life.'

The next morning, Samridhi woke up to a surprise waiting for her on the dining table—a brand-new radio, sleek and shiny.

Her father smiled as she ran her fingers over the dials.

'You more than earned it,' he said, ruffling her hair.

But to everyone's surprise, Samridhi didn't switch it on immediately.

'Thank you, Papa,' she said softly, her eyes glancing toward her homemade sound recorder. 'But I think... I'm more excited about making something new now.'

Her parents exchanged smiles as her father said, 'Looks like we have a budding inventor in the family.'

In the days that followed, Samridhi's curiosity only grew. She began experimenting with more materials, trying to refine her sound recorder and learn about how modern technology had evolved from those early devices.

As she sat at her desk one evening, sketching ideas for her next project, Samridhi realised that her love for music had opened a door to an entirely new world—one where creativity and science worked together in harmony.

And with her newfound curiosity and determination, Samridhi knew this was only the beginning of her journey.

Hypatia

Discovery: Commentary on geometry and astronomy

Hypatia was a Greek mathematician, astronomer, and philosopher who lived in Alexandria, Egypt, around 360 to 415 CE. She was one of the first well-known female scholars in history and became a respected teacher and thinker during a time when very few women had the chance to study or teach.

Hypatia worked on important ideas in mathematics, such as geometry and algebra, and helped preserve and explain the works of earlier scientists like Ptolemy and Euclid.

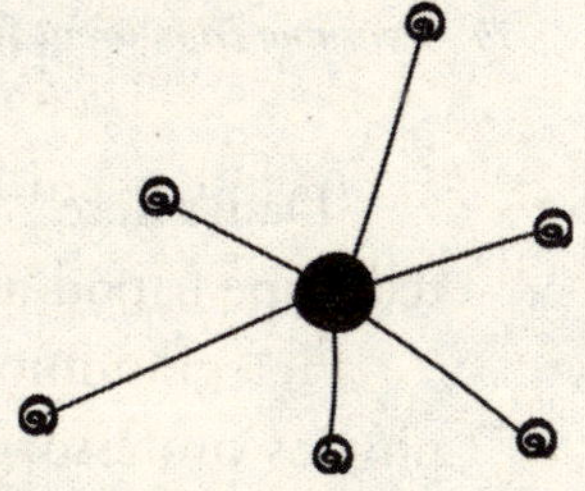

Aisha and the Star Map

The warm summer breeze carried the scent of jasmine through Aisha's open window as she lay sprawled across her bed, poring over her astronomy books. At twelve years old, she already knew more about the night sky than most adults in her neighbourhood. Her walls were plastered with star charts, and her bedside table overflowed with notebooks filled with celestial observations.

'Aisha! Come help with dinner!' her mother called from the kitchen.

'Just five more minutes, Ammi!' Aisha shouted back, her nose buried in a diagram of the Orion constellation. She was tracing the star Betelgeuse when she heard the familiar creak of the front gate. Running to the window, she saw her grandmother's taxi pulling up to their house in Mumbai.

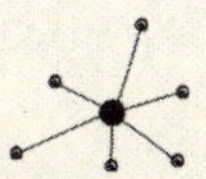

'Dadi's here!' Aisha squealed, nearly tripping over her telescope tripod in her rush downstairs.

Her grandmother, Dr Fatima Khan, was a retired physics professor who had spent her career teaching at universities across India. Though she walked with a cane now, her sharp eyes still sparkled with the same curiosity that had made her one of the most respected women in Indian academia.

'Aisha, beta!' Dadi opened her arms wide. 'Let me see how much you've grown!'

After dinner, as the family sat on the rooftop terrace enjoying the evening cool, Aisha pointed excitedly at the emerging stars. 'Look, Dadi! Venus is already visible, and Jupiter will rise soon!'

Dadi smiled knowingly. 'You remind me of someone very special—Hypatia of Alexandria. Do you know who she was?'

Aisha shook her head, her dark braids swinging.

'Over 1,600 years ago,' Dadi began, settling into her favorite wicker chair, 'Hypatia was the greatest astronomer and mathematician of her time. She studied the stars from the great Library of Alexandria, creating detailed star charts that helped sailors navigate the Mediterranean.'

As fireflies danced around them, Dadi painted a vivid picture of ancient Alexandria—its towering lighthouse, bustling markets, and the great library where Hypatia taught. She described how Hypatia used an astrolabe to measure star positions and invented a hydrometer to study liquids.

'But Dadi,' Aisha interrupted, 'how did she make star charts without telescopes?'

'With patience and mathematics,' Dadi explained. 'She would track each star's movement night after night, calculating their positions. Her work was so precise that her star maps were used for centuries.'

Aisha's eyes widened. 'Could we make our own star chart? Like Hypatia did?'

Dadi's face lit up. 'What a wonderful idea! We'll start tomorrow night.'

The next evening, they spread a large sheet of paper on the rooftop. Dadi taught Aisha how to identify reference stars and plot their positions using angular measurements. They worked for hours, Aisha carefully marking each star while Dadi shared more stories about Hypatia's life—how she defended the library against religious extremists, how she rode her chariot through Alexandria to teach both men and women, and how she was ultimately martyred for her knowledge.

'Hypatia proved that women belong in science just as much as men,' Dadi said firmly, adjusting Aisha's grip on the protractor. 'The stars don't care if you're a boy or girl—they shine the same for all who take the time to look.'

After three nights of meticulous work, Aisha completed her star map, labelling constellations in both English and the Arabic names Dadi had taught her. Just in time too—her family's annual camping trip to Lonavala was coming up.

'Can I use my map to navigate?' Aisha begged her parents.

Her father chuckled. 'As long as you don't get us lost in the jungle!'

At the campsite, far from city lights, the Milky Way blazed across the sky like a river of diamonds. Aisha spread her map on a flat rock, using a red-filtered flashlight to preserve her night vision.

'According to my calculations,' she announced importantly to her younger brother Kabir, 'that bright star near the horizon is Arcturus. If we follow it west, we should see Corona Borealis.'

Kabir rolled his eyes but followed her pointing finger. 'I just see a bunch of dots.'

Aisha sighed dramatically. 'Those 'dots' helped ancient travellers cross oceans! Hypatia's students could probably identify twenty constellations by age ten.'

Her grandmother laughed. 'Give him time, Aisha. Even the greatest astronomers started by learning one star at a time.'

As the week progressed, Aisha became the campsite's unofficial guide. Other families would gather around as she pointed out celestial wonders using her handmade map. She explained how sailors used Polaris to navigate, how the ancient Egyptians aligned their pyramids with Orion's Belt, and how Hypatia's work influenced centuries of astronomers.

On their last night, as Aisha was packing her supplies, she noticed Dadi deep in conversation with her parents near the campfire. She caught phrases like 'natural talent' and 'should nurture this.'

The morning they returned home, Aisha's father called her into the living room. There, on the coffee table, sat a long rectangular box.

'Open it,' her mother urged.

With trembling fingers, Aisha lifted the lid to reveal a gleaming Celestron telescope-the same model she'd been admiring at the science store for months.

'Dadi told us how serious you are about astronomy,' her father said, ruffling her hair. 'This belonged to her when she taught at the university.'

Aisha turned to her grandmother, who was smiling knowingly. 'Every great astronomer needs proper equipment,' Dadi said. 'Hypatia would have killed for a telescope like this.'

That night, as Aisha calibrated her new telescope on the rooftop, she thought about Hypatia studying the same stars without any instruments. She imagined the ancient scholar patiently recording each star's position night after night, just as she had done with her map.

'One day,' Aisha whispered to the stars, 'I'll make discoveries that would make you proud, Hypatia.'

In the years that followed, Aisha's childhood passion blossomed into a brilliant career. She would go on to study astrophysics at MIT, eventually leading a team that discovered three new exoplanets. But she always kept her first star map framed in her office, a reminder of the summer she learned that the night sky wasn't just something to observe—it was a legacy to continue.

Mary Anning

Discovery: Fossil discoveries (Ichthyosaur, Plesiosaur)

Mary Anning was a British fossil hunter and paleontologist who lived from 1799 to 1847. She is best known for discovering important fossils along the cliffs of Lyme Regis, England, including the first complete ichthyosaur and one of the first plesiosaur skeletons. These discoveries helped scientists learn more about prehistoric life and the history of the Earth. Even though she had little formal education, Mary taught herself about science and became an expert in identifying fossils.

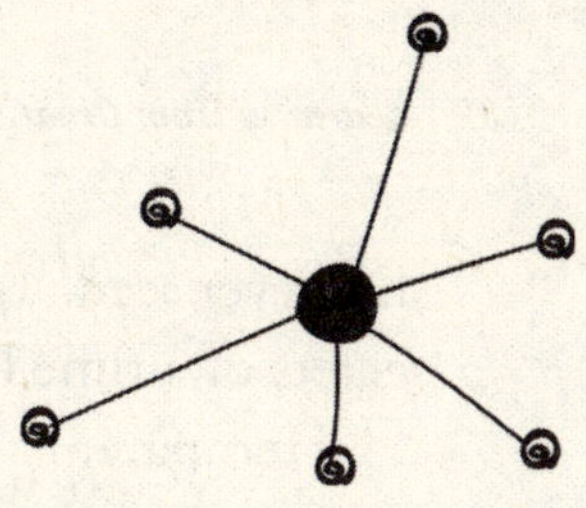

Lalita and the Ancient Fossil

The golden sands of Tarkarli beach stretched endlessly before twelve-year-old Lalita, the afternoon sun warming her back as she combed the shoreline for seashells. Her family's annual beach vacation to Maharashtra's Konkan coast was always the highlight of her summer, but this year would become truly unforgettable.

'Lali, come swim with me!' her younger brother Arjun called from the turquoise waves, his arms splashing wildly.

'In a minute!' Lalita replied absentmindedly, her attention captured by an unusual shape half-buried near a cluster of rocks. What looked like a dark, ridged stone caught her eye-but when she picked it up, her fingers traced strange, symmetrical patterns unlike any shell

she'd ever seen. The object felt heavy, ancient, whispering secrets of a time long past.

Her parents lounged under a swaying palm tree, her father reading a newspaper while her mother sorted through their picnic basket. 'Look what I found!' Lalita exclaimed, thrusting the peculiar rock toward them.

Her father adjusted his glasses, turning the object in his hands. 'Hmm…some kind of seashell fossilised into stone, perhaps?'

'Or just an oddly shaped rock,' her mother added, more interested in unpacking their lunch. 'Why don't you ask Mohan? He's lived here his whole life—if anyone would know, it's him.'

Mohan, the local guide who led fishing trips and knew every inch of the coastline, sat nearby mending a torn fishing net. His leathery hands paused as Lalita approached, her treasure extended towards him.

'Mohan-ji, do you know what this is?' she asked breathlessly.

The old fisherman's eyes widened behind his wire-rimmed glasses as he examined the specimen. A slow smile spread across his sun-weathered face. 'Lalita *beti*, do you realise what you've found? This is no ordinary stone-this is a fossil! Probably millions of years old.'

'A fossil?' Lalita gasped, her heart pounding. 'Like… from dinosaurs?'

Mohan chuckled, carefully turning the fossil over in his hands. 'Maybe not a dinosaur, but certainly from some ancient creature. See these ridges? They remind me of bone structures. This coastline was underwater long ago; home to marine reptiles and other prehistoric life.'

Lalita's mind whirled with possibilities. She was holding a piece of Earth's ancient history in her hands!

For the remainder of their vacation, Lalita became a dedicated fossil hunter. Mohan taught her how to identify promising rock formations and the telltale signs of fossilisation. Every morning at dawn, she would scour the beach while the tide was low, her eyes scanning for anything unusual. By the end of their trip, her collection included several spiral-shaped ammonites and a curious bone fragment that Mohan said might belong to an ancient fish.

When the family returned to their Pune home, Lalita rushed straight to the city library, her fossil carefully wrapped in cloth. The librarian, Mrs Deshpande, recognised the spark of scientific curiosity in the young girl's eyes.

'Looking for something special?' Mrs Deshpande asked.

'Everything you have about fossils and prehistoric life!' Lalita declared.

As she pored over books in the quiet library corner, one name kept appearing: Mary Anning. The more Lalita read about this 19th century Englishwoman, the more fascinated she became.

Mary Anning had been just a child when she began hunting fossils along the cliffs of Lyme Regis. At age twelve-Lalita's exact age-Mary and her brother Joseph discovered the first complete ichthyosaur skeleton. Despite having little formal education and facing discrimination as a woman in science, Mary taught herself anatomy, geology, and scientific illustration. Her discoveries of plesiosaurs and prehistoric fish revolutionised understanding of prehistoric life and extinction.

Lalita's fingers trembled as she turned the pages. Here was a girl like her, from humble beginnings, who changed science forever through perseverance and keen observation. The parallels were uncanny—both young girls, both making discoveries by the sea, both captivated by ancient life.

Armed with this inspiration, Lalita dove deeper into research. She learned that during the Mesozoic Era, much of India had been submerged under a shallow sea teeming with marine reptiles. The fossil she found might be from a plesiosaur or mosasaur—enormous predators that ruled prehistoric oceans.

For her next project, Lalita decided to recreate the ancient Konkan coastline as it might have looked when her fossilised creature was alive. She spent weeks crafting an elaborate diorama:

- A painted backdrop showing a tropical sea under stormy skies.
- Clay models of long-necked plesiosaurs gliding through waves.
- A toothy mosasaur lurking near the ocean floor.

Her actual fossil embedded in the 'seafloor' alongside ammonites she'd collected.

The centrepiece was a magnificent plesiosaur she sculpted from clay, its flippers outstretched as if frozen mid-swim. Lalita painstakingly painted every scale using reference images from library books, determined to make it scientifically accurate.

When she presented the finished project to her science teacher, Ms Mamta's eyes widened behind her thick glasses. 'Lalita, this is extraordinary work! The anatomical accuracy, the research behind it...' She examined the embedded fossil closely. 'And you say you found this yourself?'

Lalita nodded eagerly. 'On Tarkarli beach! Studying it led me to Mary Anning's story, which inspired this whole project.'

Ms Mamta smiled knowingly. 'We have a statewide Young Scientists Exhibition next month. I'd like you to enter this.'

The exhibition day arrived in a whirlwind of nervous excitement. Lalita stood proudly beside her diorama as judges and visitors crowded around. She explained how her fossil discovery connected to Maharashtra's prehistoric past, citing Mary Anning's similar journey from beachcombing child to celebrated fossil hunter.

'Your understanding of paleontology is impressive for someone your age,' remarked one judge, a geology professor from Pune University. 'Have you considered what kind of scientist you want to be?'

Lalita didn't hesitate. 'A paleontologist! I want to study India's prehistoric marine life and discover new species, just like Mary Anning did in England.'

After the exhibition, Ms Mamta presented Lalita with a wrapped package. Inside was a beautiful leather-bound journal and a book titled *Remarkable Women in Science: From Mary Anning to Modern Trailblazers.*

'For recording your future discoveries,' Ms Mamta said with a wink.

That night, Lalita placed her fossil on the bookshelf above her study desk, right beside the diorama. As she opened her new journal to its first page, she wrote:

'Discovery #1—Tarkarli Beach Fossil, July 2023. This is only the beginning...'

Years later, Dr Lalita Joshi would indeed become one of India's leading paleontologists. Her childhood fossil turned out to be part of a previously unknown marine reptile species from the Late Cretaceous period. When she published her groundbreaking research, she made sure to credit Mary Anning in her acknowledgments:

'To Mary Anning—the fossil hunter who proved that curiosity and perseverance can uncover lost worlds, and who inspired a young girl on a Maharashtra beach to follow in her footsteps.'

Jan Ingenhousz

Discovery: Photosynthesis

Jan Ingenhousz was a Dutch scientist and physician who lived from 1730 to 1799. He is best known for discovering that plants produce oxygen through a process called Photosynthesis. In his experiments, he found that plants only release oxygen when they are in sunlight, not in the dark. This showed that sunlight is an important part of how plants make food and give off oxygen, which is essential for life on Earth.

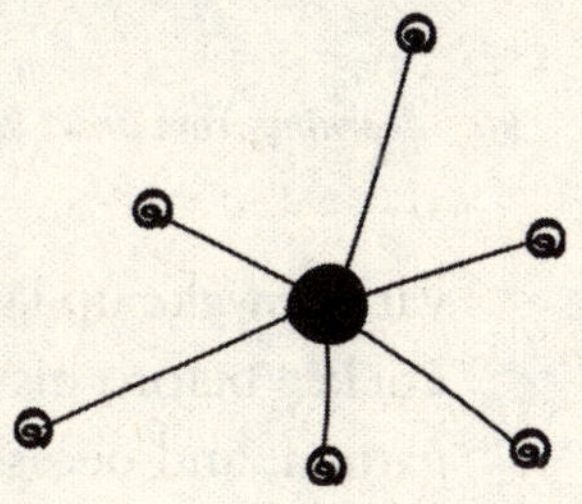

Nirmal's Lazy Garden

The afternoon sun beat down mercilessly on Nirmal's back as he scowled at the patch of dry, cracked earth his parents had designated as his 'summer project.' At fourteen, he had far more important things to do than play farmer—like perfecting his cricket bowling technique or exploring the bamboo groves with his friends.

'Just dig some holes, throw in the seeds, and be done with it,' he muttered to himself, attacking the hardened soil with his rusty trowel. The metal blade clinked against stones as sweat dripped from his forehead. After making a few token holes, he ripped open the packet of okra seeds his mother had given him and scattered them carelessly before splashing some water from the nearby well. The entire 'gardening' session lasted precisely eleven minutes—he'd timed it.

Over the next two weeks, Nirmal's routine never

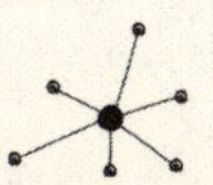

varied: wake up late, gulp down breakfast, escape to play cricket before his mother could remind him about the garden, and occasionally toss some water at the pathetic sprouts when guilt struck. The results were predictably dismal—a few spindly shoots struggling through the crusted soil, their leaves already yellowing at the edges.

One sweltering Tuesday afternoon, as Nirmal lounged in the meager shade of the Neem tree pretending to weed, his best friend Arif vaulted over the low stone wall that separated their properties. His football bounced erratically across the parched earth before coming to rest against Nirmal's sole surviving okra plant.

'Your garden looks deader than my grandfather's old radio,' Arif announced cheerfully, poking at the wilted leaves.

Nirmal shrugged. 'Plants are boring. They don't do anything except sit there looking sad.'

Arif crouched down, his brow furrowing as he examined the soil. 'Abbu says plants are actually doing incredible things we can't see. They're like tiny factories working all day.'

'Yeah? What kind of factory sits around turning brown in the sun?' Nirmal scoffed, but curiosity flickered in his eyes.

Arif grinned and grabbed his arm. 'Come on, let's ask Abbu. He was just telling me about some Dutch scientist who figured out how plants eat sunlight.'

Jamal Uncle, Arif's father and the village high school's biology teacher, was repairing fishing nets in the shaded courtyard of their home. When the boys tumbled in, breathless with questions, he set aside his work with a patient smile.

'So Nirmal wants to understand the secret life of plants?' Jamal Uncle's eyes twinkled as he led them to his bookshelf. 'Let me introduce you to Jan Ingenhousz.'

What followed was an afternoon that would change Nirmal's life. Jamal Uncle spread yellowed textbooks across the low wooden table, their pages filled with diagrams of leaves and sunlight. He described how Ingenhousz, in the late 1700s, had conducted elegant experiments with submerged plants, proving they released bubbles of oxygen only when exposed to sunlight.

'See this?' Jamal Uncle pointed to an illustration showing a plant in a glass jar. 'That's photosynthesis in action—the plant taking in sunlight, water, and air to make its own food. It's why we can breathe and eat. Without this process, life as we know it wouldn't exist.'

Nirmal's fingers traced the diagrams, his mind reeling. All this time, he'd thought plants were just passive decorations, when in reality they were performing microscopic miracles every second. The wilted okra in his garden wasn't just dying—it was starving for sunlight the way he starved for his mother's biryani.

'What if,' Nirmal said slowly, ideas crystallising, 'we built something to give my plants more sunlight? Like those glass houses rich people have?'

Jamal Uncle's face lit up. 'A miniature greenhouse! Brilliant idea!'

The next three days passed in a whirlwind of activity. Jamal Uncle helped them salvage an old window frame from the school's renovation pile. They carefully measured and sawed bamboo poles to create a frame, then mounted the glass at an angle to catch the morning sun. Nirmal, who had never shown patience for any task lasting more than twenty minutes, found himself spending hours perfecting the structure, adjusting the angle by fractions to optimise light exposure.

They transplanted the healthiest seedlings into rich new soil beneath the glass enclosure, marking control plants outside the greenhouse for comparison. Nirmal started keeping meticulous notes in a makeshift logbook—plant heights, leaf colours, even soil temperatures taken with a thermometer borrowed from Jamal Uncle's lab.

The results astonished everyone. Within a week, the greenhouse plants had doubled in size, their leaves a vibrant green compared to the stunted, yellowish control plants. Nirmal found himself waking at dawn to check on his charges, often skipping cricket matches to monitor their progress.

One evening, as Nirmal adjusted the greenhouse ventilation, his father came out to watch, his arms crossed over his chest. 'I thought you hated gardening,' he remarked, nodding at the thriving plants.

Nirmal wiped sweat from his forehead, leaving a streak of dirt. 'It's not gardening, Papa. It's…' He struggled for the right word.

'Science,' his father finished for him, a proud smile tugging at his lips.

The monsoon rains arrived early that year, threatening to destroy their experiment. Nirmal and Arif worked frantically to build a drainage system around the greenhouse, using broken tiles to divert the torrential downpour. When the skies cleared, their plants stood strong while the control group had been battered to mush.

Harvest day felt like a festival. Nirmal's mother cooked a feast using their homegrown okra, the tender pods far superior to anything from the market. As the family sat around the table savoring the fruits of his labor, Nirmal couldn't stop explaining how the greenhouse had accelerated growth by optimising photosynthetic efficiency.

His younger sister rolled her eyes. 'You've become such a science bore.'

But Nirmal just grinned, spearing another piece of okra. He didn't mind the teasing because he'd discovered something incredible—that beneath the surface of ordinary things lay extraordinary processes waiting to be understood. The same plants he'd dismissed as boring were actually complex chemical factories, silently transforming sunlight into life itself.

That night, as fireflies danced outside his window, Nirmal carefully tended to his newest experiment—a sweet potato vine growing in a jar of water. He adjusted its position to catch the moonlight, just in case. After all, who knew what other plant secrets were waiting to be discovered?

In the quiet darkness, surrounded by his thriving plants, Nirmal realised something profound. He wasn't just growing vegetables anymore. He was growing into a scientist. And this was only the beginning.

Katherine Johnson
Spaceflight trajectory calculations

Katherine Johnson was an American mathematician who lived from 1918 to 2020. She worked for NASA and played a key role in some of the most important space missions in history. Using her sharp math skills, she calculated flight paths, launch windows, and return trajectories for missions including the first American in space and the Apollo 11 moon landing. Her work helped ensure that astronauts could travel safely to space and back home again.

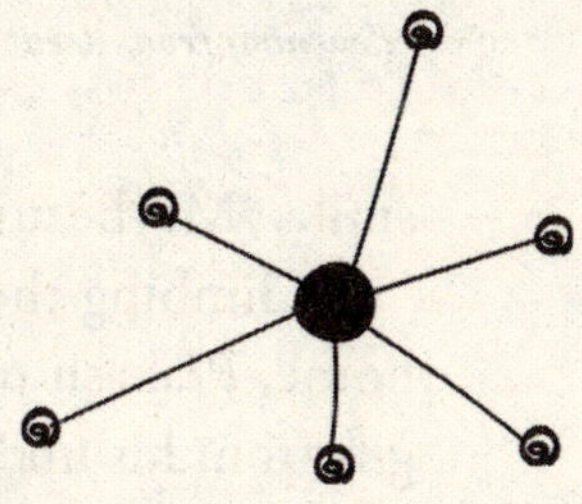

Prakash's Journey to the Stars

The dusty streets of Jaipur shimmered under the afternoon sun as fourteen-year-old Prakash raced home from school, his tattered backpack bouncing against his shoulders. He skidded to a stop outside his family's modest tailor shop, where his father sat hunched over a sewing machine, meticulously stitching golden thread into an elaborate wedding sherwani.

'Papa! The Falcon Heavy is launching in twenty minutes!' Prakash announced breathlessly, wiping sweat from his forehead.

His father barely glanced up from his work. 'Not now, beta. Mrs Sharma's order must be ready by evening.'

Prakash's shoulders slumped. He had watched every SpaceX and ISRO launch for the past three years, but no one in his family understood his fascination. His mother, busy measuring fabric nearby, gave him an apologetic

smile. 'Maybe after dinner, son.'

Climbing the narrow staircase to their small rooftop home, Prakash pulled out his secondhand smartphone a gift from his uncle last Diwali and tuned into the NASA livestream. As the countdown reached zero, he held his breath, watching the massive rocket tear through the atmosphere with earth-shaking power. In that moment, surrounded by the smell of his mother's cooking wafting from downstairs, Prakash felt the familiar ache in his chest. He didn't just want to watch rockets—he wanted to build them, to understand the physics that could hurl metal and dreams beyond the sky.

At school the next day, Prakash's hand shot up during physics class. 'Sir, how exactly do rockets overcome Earth's gravity well?'

Mr Sharma, their exhausted-looking teacher, sighed and adjusted his glasses. 'That's not in your syllabus, Prakash. Focus on the problems I've written on the board.'

Prakash opened his mouth to protest when a quiet voice beside him muttered, 'It's about achieving escape velocity of 11.2 km/s, but the real trick is the thrust-to-weight ratio.'

Turning, Prakash met the knowing gaze of Arjun, the quiet boy who always sat in the back with his nose buried in advanced physics books. Their eyes locked in silent understanding.

That afternoon, Prakash lingered after school, finding Arjun reading under the banyan tree. 'You know about rocket science?'

Arjun shrugged. 'I know what I read. The school library has some old NASA publications.' He hesitated before adding, 'There's a new science museum opening near Sindhi Camp. They might have better resources.'

Prakash's heart raced. A museum! He'd never been to one. That Saturday, after helping his father deliver finished garments, he took the bus across town, his pocket heavy with saved-up allowance.

The Rajasthan Science Explorium smelled of new paint and possibility. Prakash wandered through exhibits on electricity and genetics until he found it - the Space Exploration wing. His fingers trembled as he touched a real fragment of meteorite, its surface pitted with cosmic scars. Then he saw her.

A large portrait showed a Black woman with careful curls and a determined gaze, standing before a chalkboard dense with equations. The placard read: 'Katherine Johnson, NASA Mathematician—Calculated Trajectories for America's First Spaceflights.'

Prakash stood transfixed as an elderly museum guide explained how Johnson had computed the path for Alan Shepard's 1961 spaceflight using nothing but her mathematical genius and a mechanical calculator. 'The astronauts wouldn't fly unless she checked the numbers,' the guide said with a chuckle.

Something clicked in Prakash's mind. Mathematics wasn't just abstract numbers—it was the language of the stars. He spent hours that day studying the orbital mechanics exhibit, scribbling notes in the margins of his school notebook.

That evening, Prakash burst into Arjun's home without knocking. 'We're building a rocket!'

Arjun's mother, used to her son's eccentric friends, simply sighed and brought them snacks as Prakash spread his notes across the floor. 'Not just any rocket—one where we calculate the trajectory first, like Katherine Johnson did!'

Over the next month, the boys became fixtures at the science museum, spending every free moment studying propulsion systems and fluid dynamics. They scavenged materials—balsa wood from a carpenter's scraps, a small engine from a discarded model plane, even the aluminum foil from Prakash's mother's kitchen. Their test launches in the empty lot behind Arjun's house drew crowds of neighbourhood children and more than a few complaints about noise.

Then came their breakthrough. Prakash had been puzzling over their rocket's instability during ascent when he remembered an exhibit on fin design. Racing back to the museum, he convinced the staff to let him examine the model rockets again. That night, he redesigned their prototype with subtly angled fins that induced stabilising spin.

The next test flight arced perfectly into the evening sky, a tiny dot of fire against the purple twilight before the parachute deployed. The neighbourhood children cheered as it drifted down. Even Arjun, usually so reserved, whooped with joy.

'You should show this to Dr Singh,' Arjun said

suddenly as they packed up their equipment.

'Who?'

'The museum director. He came by last week when you were at your father's shop. Asked about our project.'

Prakash's stomach fluttered. Present their amateur rocket to an actual scientist? But Katherine Johnson's face flashed in his memory—a woman who walked into rooms where no one believed she belonged.

Dr Singh turned out to be a tall, serious man with salt-and-pepper hair and sharp eyes that missed nothing. He examined their rocket with surprising care, asking pointed questions about their calculations. Prakash's palms sweated as he explained their thrust calculations, but his voice grew stronger as he saw the director's approving nods.

When Prakash mentioned Katherine Johnson's influence, Dr Singh's eyes lit up. 'Ah! You know she recalculated John Glenn's orbital trajectory by hand when the computers failed?' He leaned forward. 'Prakash, how would you like to attend the International Youth Space Program this summer?'

Prakash nearly dropped his notebook. 'The... the NASA one?'

Dr Singh smiled. 'The very same. The museum sponsors one student annually, and I think we've found our candidate.'

The bus ride home passed in a blur. Prakash's mind raced with how to break the news to his parents. Would they understand? Would they even let him go?

To his astonishment, his father set aside his sewing that evening and listened intently as Prakash explained the opportunity. His mother's eyes shone with tears as she ran her fingers over the rocket model.

'All this time,' his father murmured, 'I thought you were just playing.' He reached into a locked drawer and pulled out a yellowed photograph. 'My grandfather worked on the railway engines that carried parts for India's first rocket launches. He used to tell me stories...'

Prakash stared at the photo of a young man standing proudly beside a massive train cargo. The family resemblance was unmistakable.

His father squeezed his shoulder. 'We may be tailors now, but the stars call to whom they call. You'll go to America, beta. We'll make it work.'

On the day of his departure, Prakash stood at the airport with his rocket model carefully packed in his luggage. Arjun pressed a book into his hands— 'Fundamentals of Astrodynamics' with a note inside: 'For when you calculate your own moon landing.'

As the plane roared down the runway, Prakash pressed his forehead to the window, watching India shrink below him. Somewhere ahead lay NASA, calculus, and the endless stars. And somewhere behind, in a small tailor's shop in Jaipur, his parents would be waiting—their eyes turned upward, finally understanding the sky that had always called to their son.

The journey ahead would be long, but Prakash knew the truth now: no dream was too distant when you had the right equations. And thanks to a woman who once calculated paths to the stars with pencil and paper, he knew exactly how to plot his course.

Alan Turing

Invention: Codebreaking; foundations of computing

Alan Turing was a British mathematician, computer scientist, and codebreaker who lived from 1912 to 1954. He is best known for helping to break the German Enigma code during World War II, which played a major role in helping the Allies win the war. Turing designed a special machine that could quickly go through many possible code combinations, which saved countless lives by uncovering enemy plans.

Turing is also considered one of the fathers of modern computer science.

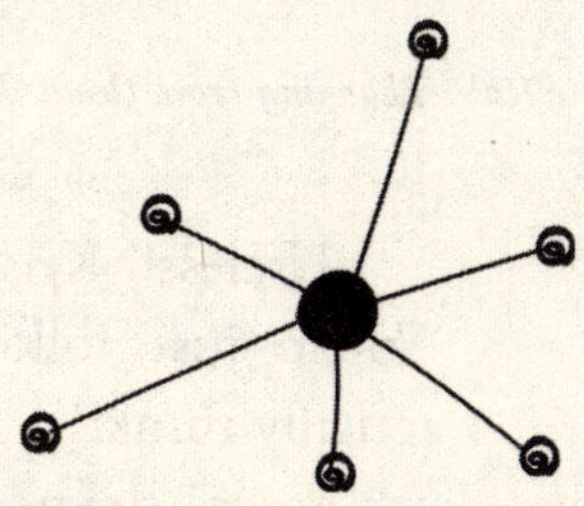

Krishna and the
Thinking Machine

The afternoon sun streamed through Krishna's bedroom window, illuminating the chaos of his latest project. At twelve years old, he had already transformed his space into something resembling a mad scientist's laboratory. The shelves groaned under the weight of robotics manuals, half-assembled circuit boards, and three generations of homemade robots—each slightly more functional than the last. His mother had stopped complaining about the mess months ago, though she still occasionally tripped over loose wires when bringing in his afternoon snack.

Krishna sat hunched over his fourth robot attempt, a small rover meant to navigate using basic artificial intelligence. He adjusted the sensor array with careful fingers, his dark brows furrowed in concentration. The robot whirred to life, took three jerky steps forward, then promptly veered off course and crashed into his bookshelf.

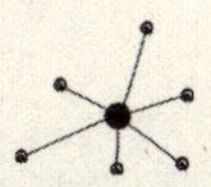

'Useless!' Krishna groaned, flopping onto his back. 'You're just following programming. I want you to actually think!'

Across town, his best friend Joy was having a very different afternoon. 'You have to come over tomorrow,' Joy insisted during their video call, his face pixelated on Krishna's laptop screen. 'Abba just finished his new AI project. It's incredible!'

Krishna's heart leapt. Joy's father, David Uncle, was a senior engineer at one of Bangalore's top tech firms. If anyone could help him understand real artificial intelligence, it was him.

The next day, Krishna practically vibrated with excitement as he pedaled his bicycle through Bangalore's bustling streets. The city hummed around him—auto-rickshaws weaving through traffic, street vendors calling out their wares, the ever-present scent of masala dosa in the air. But Krishna barely noticed. His mind was already in Joy's home office, imagining the technological marvels waiting for him.

David Uncle's workspace was exactly as Krishna had dreamed—a temple of technology with multiple monitors displaying lines of code, shelves filled with technical manuals, and an impressive array of computer hardware. The centrepiece was a large screen displaying a simple chat interface:

> Hello! I'm Nova. How can I help you today?

'Is this...?' Krishna's voice caught in his throat.

'A basic AI chatbot,' David Uncle confirmed, his

eyes twinkling behind rectangular glasses. 'Nothing like what you see in movies, but it can hold surprisingly complex conversations.'

Krishna's fingers hovered over the keyboard. 'Does it actually understand me?'

David Uncle pulled up a chair. 'That's the million-dollar question. Let me tell you about the man who first asked it.'

What followed was the most fascinating afternoon of Krishna's life. David Uncle spoke of Alan Turing—the brilliant British mathematician who had cracked Nazi codes during World War II and later proposed the famous Turing Test.

'He imagined a future where we'd ask: can machines think?' David Uncle explained. 'Not just calculate or follow instructions, but truly reason and learn.'

Krishna's mind raced ahead. 'And your chatbot... is it close to passing the Turing Test?'

David Uncle laughed, a rich, warm sound. 'Not even remotely! But the principles are the same. We're teaching machines to learn patterns, to respond appropriately, to —in a very limited way understand.'

That night, Krishna lay awake staring at his ceiling, Turing's words echoing in his mind. Could he create something that learned? Not just another pre-programmed robot, but a system that grew smarter over time?

By sunrise, he had a plan.

The next two weeks passed in a blur of code and caffeine. Krishna commandeered the family computer (much to his sister's annoyance) and spent every free moment studying machine learning tutorials online. He pestered David Uncle with increasingly technical questions until even the engineer had to occasionally say, 'I'll get back to you on that one.'

His first attempts were disastrous. A weather predictor that always forecast rain. A joke-telling algorithm that generated nonsense like 'Why did the chicken cross the road? Because seven ate nine.' But Krishna persisted, rewriting, testing, improving.

Then came the breakthrough.

> Hello! I'm K-Bot. What would you like to teach me today?

It was simple—painfully so by professional standards—but it worked. The program could store facts and recall them later, learning from each interaction.

Joy came over to test it, his skepticism quickly turning to amazement. 'You built this? From scratch?'

Krishna nodded, watching anxiously as Joy typed:

> The capital of France is Paris.
> K-Bot: I understand. The capital of France is Paris.
> What is the capital of France?
> K-Bot: The capital of France is Paris.

Joy's eyes widened. 'It remembers!'

'It learns,' Krishna corrected, his voice trembling with excitement.

When David Uncle came to visit that weekend, Krishna demonstrated K-Bot with sweaty palms. The program wasn't perfect—it struggled with abstract concepts and occasionally gave hilariously wrong answers —but it undeniably improved with each interaction.

David watched in silence as K-Bot recalled facts, answered questions, and even attempted (poorly) to tell a joke. When the demonstration ended, the engineer removed his glasses and rubbed his eyes.

'Krishna,' he said finally, 'do you understand what you've accomplished here?'

Krishna shifted nervously. 'It's just a simple learning algorithm...'

'It's a neural network prototype!' David exclaimed. 'You've created a self-improving system with no formal training!' He turned to Krishna's parents. 'Do you realise how remarkable this is? Most university students struggle with these concepts.'

Krishna's mother beamed with pride while his father—usually reserved about Krishna's 'hobby'—clapped him on the shoulder. 'Maybe we should get you a better computer,' he murmured.

That night, as Krishna lay in bed, he imagined Alan Turing looking down from some celestial computer lab, smiling at this Indian boy who had taken up his challenge. The road ahead was long—K-Bot was still lightyears away from true AI—but the foundation was there.

Somewhere in Bangalore, in a modest home filled with love and half-built robots, the future of artificial intelligence was taking shape—one line of code at a time.

Five Years Later....

The auditorium at the Indian Institute of Science buzzed with anticipation as nineteen-year-old Krishna Mukherjee approached the podium. His paper, 'Adaptive

Learning Algorithms for Resource-Constrained Environments,' had just won the prestigious Turing Young Innovator Award.

As he adjusted the microphone, his eyes found David Uncle and Joy in the front row, beaming with pride. Behind them sat his parents, their faces glowing with a mixture of awe and incomprehension—they still didn't quite understand his work, but they knew it was changing lives.

Krishna took a deep breath and began:

'When I was twelve years old, I asked a simple question: can machines learn? Today, I stand here because someone once asked that question before me...'

The audience leaned forward as Krishna's story unfolded—of a curious boy, a mentor's guidance, and the timeless legacy of Alan Turing. Somewhere in the back, a first-year computer science student wiped away tears, her own dreams suddenly feeling within reach.

And in Krishna's pocket, on his smartphone, a simple app hummed quietly—the great-great-grandchild of K-Bot, still learning, still growing, still answering the eternal question: Can machines think?

The answer, it seemed, was yes.

Wilhelm Conrad Röntgen

Invention: Discovery of X-rays

Wilhelm Conrad Röntgen was a German physicist who lived from 1845 to 1923. He is best known for discovering X-rays in 1895, a breakthrough that changed medicine forever.

Röntgen's discovery allowed doctors to see inside the human body without surgery, making it easier to diagnose injuries and illnesses. For this important work, he received the very first Nobel Prize in Physics in 1901.

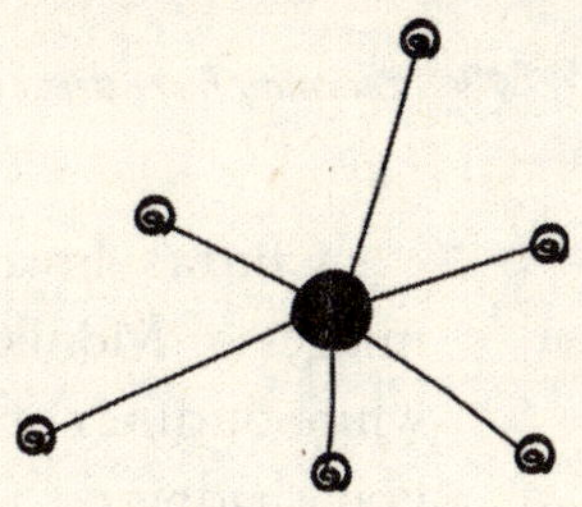

Chitra and the Invisible Light

The rhythmic beeping of hospital machines still echoed in Chitra's ears as she walked home from the bus stop, the scent of antiseptic lingering in her clothes. Her best friend Monika had finally been discharged after a week-long stay for severe abdominal pain, and though the doctors said it was just a nasty infection, seeing her usually energetic friend so weak had left Chitra unsettled.

'Come visit tomorrow,' Monika had whispered as they helped her into the car, her fingers surprisingly strong around Chitra's wrist. 'I have something amazing to show you.'

The next afternoon, Chitra found Monika sprawled on the living room couch, flipping through a large manila envelope with a mischievous grin. 'Look what they gave me before discharging me!' Monika pulled out several dark plastic sheets, holding them up to the light.

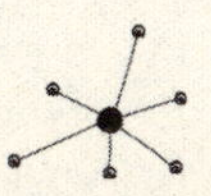

Chitra's breath caught. They were X-rays—actual images of Monika's own abdomen, showing the ghostly white outlines of her pelvis and spine floating in a sea of gray shadows.

'You can see my bones right through me,' Monika said, tracing the shapes with her finger. The faint outline of what looked like a safety pin glowed near her hip. 'That's the clip they used during my appendectomy last year.'

Chitra took the films with trembling hands, marveling at how they revealed the hidden architecture of her friend's body. 'How does this even work?' she murmured, tilting the image to catch more light.

Monika shrugged. 'Magic science camera? I was too drugged up to ask.'

That evening, Chitra sat cross-legged on her bed, staring at the ceiling. The X-ray images haunted her—not in a scary way, but like an unsolved riddle. How could light pass through flesh but not bone? What kind of camera could see inside a person?

Her laptop screen glowed in the dark room as she typed 'How do X-rays work?' The search results led her down a rabbit hole of physics and medical history, until she stumbled upon a grainy black-and-white photograph of a serious-looking man with a bushy mustache and intense eyes: Wilhelm Conrad Röntgen.

The story unfolded like something from a detective novel. In 1895, the German physicist was experimenting with cathode rays in his laboratory when he noticed something extraordinary—a chemically coated screen across the room began to glow, even though his apparatus was covered with thick black cardboard. Some unknown type of ray was passing through solid objects!

Chitra's heart raced as she read how Röntgen spent the next seven weeks locked in his lab, systematically testing the properties of these mysterious 'X-rays' (X for unknown). He discovered they could pass through human tissue but were blocked by denser materials like bone or metal. The first X-ray image ever taken was of his wife Anna Bertha's hand—the bones and her wedding ring clearly visible in the eerie photograph that would revolutionise medicine.

'But how?' Chitra whispered to the empty room. She needed to understand, not just read about it.

The next morning, Chitra arrived at Monika's house carrying a box full of supplies she'd gathered from around her home: a powerful flashlight, sheets of paper, aluminum foil, black construction paper, her little brother's plastic skeleton model, and a blank white sheet to serve as their 'film.'

'What's all this?' Monika asked, peering into the box as they settled on her sunlit balcony.

'An experiment,' Chitra said, her fingers trembling with excitement as she arranged their materials. 'We're going to understand how X-rays work.'

She taped the plastic skeleton to the balcony railing and positioned the white sheet behind it. 'Okay, so X-rays are a type of light we can't see,' Chitra explained, switching on the flashlight. 'They pass through soft tissues but get blocked by dense things like bones.'

First, she shone the light through a plain sheet of paper onto their 'film.' The paper barely dimmed the light at all. 'See? Like how X-rays go right through skin and muscle.'

Next came the aluminum foil. Only faint light penetrated the metal, casting a dull glow on their sheet. 'This is like how X-rays are partially blocked by organs and fluids.'

Finally, the black construction paper stopped nearly all the light. 'And this,' Chitra said triumphantly, 'is like your bones!'

Monika's eyes widened. 'So in a real X-ray machine, the bones show up white because they're blocking the rays from reaching the film?'

'Exactly!' Chitra's grin nearly split her face. 'The X-ray film starts out all white, and where the rays hit it, it turns dark. So the bones stay white because no rays get through to expose those parts!'

Monika's mother, a high school biology teacher, came out to see what all the excitement was about. She watched their demonstration with growing amazement. 'You've essentially recreated Röntgen's basic discovery!' Mrs Sharma said, adjusting her glasses. 'Though real X-ray machines use special detectors instead of our eyes to capture the images.'

She went inside and returned with her laptop, showing them modern CT and MRI scans that built upon Röntgen's discovery. 'Now we can see slices through the body in any direction, or even make 3D models of someone's insides.'

That night, Chitra lay awake staring at the glow-in-the-dark stars on her ceiling, now imagining them as X-rays streaming through space. One man's curiosity had opened a window into the human body that saved countless lives. Because of Röntgen's accidental discovery, doctors could diagnose broken bones, find tumors, even watch babies developing in the womb—all without making a single incision.

At school the next week, Chitra presented her X-ray experiments to the science club. As she showed Monika's actual X-rays (with personal details carefully covered), she saw her classmates lean forward, their faces reflecting the same wonder she'd felt.

'Next time any of you get an X-ray,' Chitra concluded, holding up the image of Röntgen she'd printed, 'remember you're seeing the world through his invisible light.'

Monika, now fully recovered, grinned from the front row and gave her a thumbs-up. In that moment, Chitra realised science wasn't just facts in textbooks— it was the spark of curiosity that leads to discoveries changing how we see our world, both inside and out.

Ten Years Later...

Dr Chitra Menon adjusted the lead apron around her patient's waist. 'Just hold still for one second,' she said soothingly as she positioned the digital X-ray sensor.

The elderly woman smiled nervously. 'Will it hurt?'

'Not at all,' Chitra assured her. 'It's just like having your photograph taken.'

As she stepped behind the protective screen and pressed the button, the machine emitted its familiar whir. On the monitor, the woman's hip joint materialised in shades of gray and white—the ball-and-socket structure clearly visible beneath layers of muscle and fat.

Chitra studied the image with a practiced eye, noting the hairline fracture in the femoral neck. Her fingers automatically went to the small silver pendant she always wore—a replica of Anna Bertha Röntgen's hand

X-ray, the first ever taken.

'Everything okay, doctor?' the patient asked anxiously.

Chitra smiled. 'Just a small crack. We'll have you fixed up in no time.'

As she helped the woman to the examination room, Chitra's mind drifted back to that afternoon on Monika's balcony, when two curious girls had unraveled the mystery of X-rays with nothing but a flashlight and some paper. Who would have guessed that simple experiment would light the path to medical school?

In the break room later, a first-year resident paged through an old journal article about Wilhelm Röntgen. 'Can you imagine discovering something like that by accident?' he marveled.

Chitra sipped her coffee, her eyes twinkling. 'Oh, I can imagine it perfectly.'

For in the end, wasn't all of medicine built upon such moments of wonder? The sudden realisations, the happy accidents, the relentless human curiosity that keeps pushing back the boundaries of what we can see and understand.

And as the X-ray machine hummed softly in the next room, ready to reveal another hidden truth, Chitra knew Röntgen's invisible light would keep illuminating the way forward.

Erwin Schrödinger

Schrödinger equation; Quantum theory

Erwin Schrödinger was an Austrian physicist who lived from 1887 to 1961. He is best known for his work in quantum mechanics, especially for creating the Schrödinger equation, which helps scientists understand how very small particles like electrons behave.

Schrödinger is also famous for a thought experiment called "Schrödinger's cat," which he used to show how strange quantum physics can be. In this experiment, a cat in a box is both alive and dead at the same time—until someone opens the box to check.

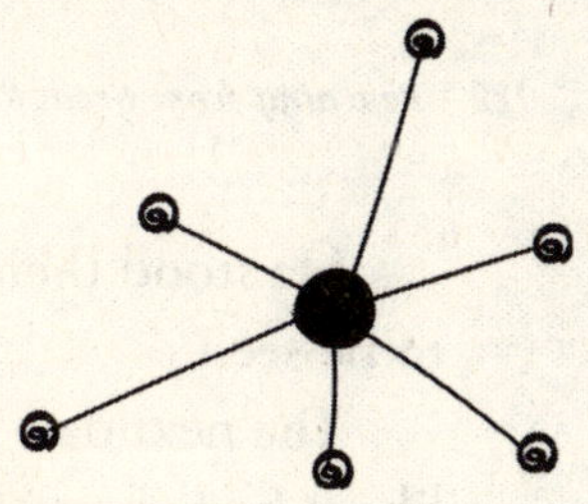

Kabir and the Curious Case
of Schrödinger's Cat

Kabir Mehta was not the kind of boy who believed in magic. He liked facts, logic, and science—things that made sense. So when a scruffy, grey-and-white stray cat started appearing and disappearing around his neighbourhood, Kabir was more confused than impressed.

It started one evening when he was taking out the garbage. As he walked back toward the house, a soft meow echoed from the bushes near the gate.

'Hello?' Kabir knelt down and saw a pair of green eyes staring back at him.

The cat was thin but not sickly, its fur matted and dirty. It blinked at Kabir, tilted its head, and then...

Poof.

It was gone.

'Whoa!' Kabir blinked, rubbing his eyes. 'Did... did that cat just vanish?'

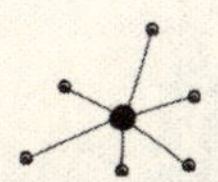

He stood there, bewildered, but the cat was nowhere to be seen.

The next day, the cat was back—sitting on the porch like it had always belonged there.

'Okay... this is weird,' Kabir muttered, crouching down again.

'Where did you go yesterday?' he asked, scratching the cat's head gently. The cat purred, rubbing its head against his hand, then meowed softly as if in reply.

'Alright, you can stay,' Kabir decided. 'But I'm going to figure you out.'

He scooped up the cat and brought it inside.

'Hmm...' Kabir studied the cat's inquisitive face. 'You disappear and reappear whenever you want. I'm calling you Schrödinger.'

The cat blinked as if approving the name.

For the next few days, Kabir kept an eye on Schrödinger. But things only got stranger.

Sometimes, he would find Schrödinger lounging in his room. Other times, the cat would vanish for hours, only to reappear as if nothing had happened.

Once, Kabir even tried locking his door with Schrödinger inside, but when he returned—poof! The cat was gone, sitting outside on the porch like it had been waiting for him.

'Okay, this is definitely not normal,' Kabir mumbled.

Kabir knew he couldn't solve this mystery alone. So, the next day at school, he told his best friends, Hatim and Prateek, everything.

'Wait, wait, wait...' Hatim raised a hand. 'You're telling me your cat disappears? Like... *disappears* disappears?'

'Yes!' Kabir exclaimed. 'And it's not just me. I've tried locking him inside, but he still vanishes.'

Prateek leaned back in his chair, arms crossed. 'That sounds impossible.'

'Exactly!' Kabir said. 'Which is why I need your help.'

Hatim's eyes gleamed with curiosity. 'Alright, I'm in. Let's solve this.'

Prateek nodded, though he looked skeptical. 'Fine. But if it turns out you're imagining things, you owe me a pizza.'

The three friends gathered at Kabir's house that afternoon. Schrödinger, of course, was nowhere to be seen.

'Okay,' Hatim said, pulling out his tablet. 'Let's think logically. What do we know?'

Kabir paced the room.

'Schrödinger disappears and reappears randomly,' he said.

'Like a... ghost?' Prateek offered.

'Or...' Hatim's eyes lit up. 'Like a particle!'

Kabir frowned. 'A particle?'

Hatim nodded excitedly. 'Remember that thing we learned in physics last term? Quantum mechanics? Particles can exist in two states at the same time. It's called *superposition*.'

Prateek raised an eyebrow. 'Super... what?'

Hatim grinned. 'Superposition. It means something can be in multiple places at once—like light being both a particle and a wave.'

Kabir's eyes widened.

'Wait...' He looked at Hatim, his mind racing. 'Are you saying... Schrödinger's like... a quantum particle?'

Hatim shrugged. 'Maybe. I mean... you did name him *Schrödinger*. And remember the famous thought experiment? Schrödinger's cat?'

Prateek's forehead creased. 'Wasn't that the thing with the cat that was... dead and alive at the same time?'

'Exactly!' Hatim said. 'Schrödinger's cat was a thought experiment by Erwin Schrödinger. It showed how a cat inside a box could be both alive and dead until someone opened the box and looked.'

Kabir's mouth went dry. 'So... you're saying my cat might actually be... existing in two states?'

Hatim shrugged again. 'I mean... it's a theory.'

The boys spent the next few days buried in research. They read everything they could find on quantum mechanics, from Einstein's work on the photoelectric effect to Heisenberg's uncertainty principle.

'Einstein didn't like the idea of quantum superposition,' Kabir said one afternoon, flipping through another book. 'He called it *spooky action at a distance*.'

'Spooky is right,' Prateek muttered, eyeing Schrödinger, who was lazily grooming himself by the window.

'Einstein believed in determinism,' Hatim added. 'He thought everything in the universe followed strict laws—no randomness, no uncertainty.'

'But Schrödinger's experiment showed that quantum particles... and maybe even cats,' Kabir glanced at his feline friend, 'don't follow those rules.'

Schrödinger looked up as if he understood exactly what they were saying.

'We need to test this,' Kabir said one evening.

'Test what?' Hatim asked.

'If Schrödinger really exists in two states,' Kabir said, his eyes gleaming with excitement, 'we should be able to observe it.'

The boys devised a simple experiment.

They placed Schrödinger in Kabir's room and set up a webcam to record. Then they left the house, locking the door behind them.

'If he's really following quantum rules,' Kabir said, 'we should see something strange.'

When the boys returned and checked the footage, they couldn't believe their eyes.

The video showed Schrödinger sitting calmly on Kabir's bed. But at one point—just for a split second—

the cat seemed to *flicker*.

'Did you see that?' Hatim exclaimed, rewinding the footage.

They watched again. Schrödinger seemed to vanish for a fraction of a second, reappearing in the exact same spot.

Kabir's jaw dropped.

'He... he's existing in two states!'

Hatim grinned. 'Looks like your cat really is a quantum mystery.'

Over the next few days, the boys documented everything. They noted when and where Schrödinger disappeared and reappeared, keeping detailed records.

Kabir even built a small corner in his room lined with foil and mirrors, trying to simulate the conditions of a quantum experiment.

Surprisingly, Schrödinger seemed... happier.

'I think he likes being observed,' Kabir murmured one evening, watching Schrödinger purr contentedly.

'Maybe because... you're collapsing his wave function,' Hatim said with a grin.

'Collapsing his what now?' Prateek asked, confused.

'Wave function,' Hatim explained. 'In quantum physics, observing a particle—or a cat—collapses its wave function, forcing it to choose one state.'

Kabir smiled softly, scratching behind Schrödinger's ears.

'Maybe he just likes knowing someone's paying attention.'

Life with Schrödinger settled into a new rhythm. He still disappeared now and then, but Kabir no longer panicked when he couldn't find him.

Instead, he smiled, knowing that somewhere—in some quantum state—Schrödinger was always there.

One afternoon, as the boys sat in Kabir's room, Schrödinger curled up by the window.

'So,' Prateek asked, 'what's next? Do we write a paper? Become famous?'

Kabir chuckled.

'Nah,' he said, glancing fondly at his cat. 'I think I'll just enjoy having the coolest quantum cat in the universe.'

Schrödinger purred softly, as if approving the idea.

Because sometimes, the greatest mysteries weren't meant to be solved.

They were meant to be cherished.

Edmond Becquerel
Discovery: Photovoltaic effect

Edmond Becquerel was a French physicist who lived from 1820 to 1891. He is best known for discovering the photovoltaic effect in 1839, which is the basic principle behind how solar panels work.

While experimenting with an electric cell, he found that light could create an electric current—an important discovery that helped lay the foundation for solar energy technology.

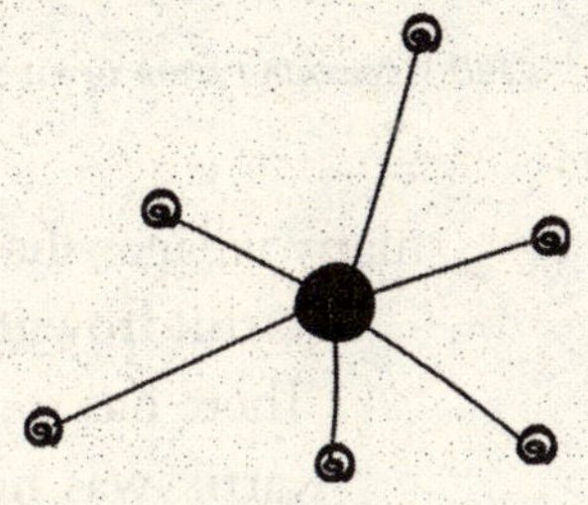

Kartik and the Power of the Sun

The summer heat was relentless in Kartik's village of Rampur. The sun beat down mercilessly, making the tin roofs of the houses hot enough to fry an egg. The worst part, however, was the frequent power cuts.

Every afternoon, just when the heat became unbearable, the ceiling fans would sputter to a stop, and the lights would flicker off. The villagers would sit outside, fanning themselves with newspapers, waiting for the electricity to return.

Kartik hated those power cuts.

'Why does the power go out all the time, Papa?' he asked one afternoon, as he and his father sat under the banyan tree, wiping sweat from their faces.

His father sighed, looking out at the fields beyond their house.

'The power supply here is unreliable,' he said. 'Too

many villages sharing too little electricity.'

Kartik frowned, his mind already racing with ideas.

'There has to be a solution,' he muttered.

Kartik was not the kind of boy who gave up easily. He loved fixing things—whether it was a leaky tap or his cousin's broken toy. But solving the village's electricity problem was a bigger challenge.

Later that evening, as he sat in his room, fanning himself with an old notebook, an idea struck him.

'If we can't get enough electricity... maybe we can make our own!'

But how?

Kartik rushed to the small library near the village school the next morning. He flipped through books on electricity, scanning the pages for answers. It was there that he stumbled upon the name Edmond Becquerel.

Kartik's eyes lit up as he read about how, in 1839, a young French scientist named Edmond Becquerel had discovered something remarkable—the photovoltaic effect.

'He found out that light could generate electricity!' Kartik murmured, fascinated.

Becquerel's discovery eventually led to the invention of solar panels—devices that could convert sunlight into electricity.

'The sun... we have plenty of that here!'

Kartik's mind buzzed with excitement. If he could harness the power of the sun, he could solve the village's power problem.

Kartik knew he couldn't do this alone. He needed help, and there was no one better to turn to than his best friend, Gautam.

Gautam was a whiz with circuits and wires. He loved tinkering with gadgets and often helped the village electrician with small repairs.

'Kartik, solar panels?' Gautam asked, raising an eyebrow when Kartik explained his idea.

'Yes!' Kartik said, his eyes gleaming. 'If we can build a mini solar panel, we can power a fan during the power cuts. Imagine how much easier summer would be for everyone!'

Gautam scratched his head, looking thoughtful. 'It's not impossible... but we'll need materials. And... we need to learn how solar panels work.'

Kartik grinned. 'I've already started reading about it. And I know where we can get some materials.'

The next few days were a whirlwind of research and learning. Kartik and Gautam pored over books and watched videos at the school's computer lab, soaking up everything they could about solar power.

'Okay,' Gautam said one evening, sitting cross-legged on Kartik's porch. 'Here's how it works. Solar panels have cells made of silicon. When sunlight hits the cells, it knocks electrons loose, creating an electric current.'

Kartik nodded eagerly. 'And we can store that electricity in a battery!'

'Exactly,' Gautam said. 'But we need to be careful. Even a small mistake can mess up the wiring.'

Kartik's confidence grew with each passing day. He was ready to put his plan into action.

Kartik and Gautam set out to gather everything they needed.

They collected:
- Broken solar garden lights from the village scrap yard, salvaging the tiny solar panels.
- Old rechargeable batteries from discarded mobile phones.
- Copper wires and small fans from the local repair shop.
- Plastic sheets and wooden frames to protect their solar cells.

The village electrician, Mr Mishra, was intrigued when the boys told him about their project.

'Trying to harness the power of the sun, are we?' he chuckled. 'Good. I'll help you with the wiring.'

With Mr Mishra's guidance, the boys learned how to solder connections and connect the solar cells to a battery.

The next weekend, Kartik and Gautam set up a small workspace under the banyan tree. They carefully arranged the solar cells in neat rows on a wooden frame, securing them with plastic sheets to protect them from dust and rain.

'Make sure the wiring is tight,' Gautam reminded Kartik as they connected the cells to the battery.

After hours of meticulous work, the mini solar panel was ready.

'Now for the moment of truth,' Kartik said, wiping his brow.

They placed the panel in direct sunlight and connected it to a small fan.

For a few seconds, nothing happened.

And then—

Whirrrrrr!

The fan spun to life, sending a cool breeze over their sweaty faces.

'We did it!' Gautam shouted, pumping his fist in the air.

Kartik beamed with pride, feeling the cool air brush against his skin.

Over the next week, the boys tested their mini solar panel tirelessly.

During the hottest part of the day, they placed it outside to charge the battery. By evening, when the power cuts started, they connected the battery to the fan.

It worked like a charm.

But Kartik wasn't satisfied yet.

'Gautam,' he said one evening, 'if we can power a fan... what else can we do?'

Gautam's eyes gleamed with excitement. 'What if we make more panels? We could power lights too!'

Word spread quickly about Kartik and Gautam's solar experiment. Soon, curious neighbors gathered under the banyan tree to see the boys' creation.

'Solar power?' Mrs Verma, their neighbour, asked, watching the fan spin. 'Can this really work for the whole village?'

Kartik's father, who had been quietly observing their work, spoke up.

'If two boys can power a fan,' he said with a smile, 'imagine what we could do if we all worked together.'

Inspired by the boys' success, the villagers came together. They pooled resources, and with the help of Mr Mishra and some donations from nearby towns, they purchased larger solar panels.

Over the next few months, Rampur transformed. Solar panels adorned rooftops, and battery-powered lights illuminated homes during power cuts.

One evening, as the sun dipped below the horizon, Kartik stood outside, watching the lights flicker on around the village.

The power cuts no longer plunged Rampur into darkness. The village was brighter, cooler, and more hopeful.

Gautam joined him, a proud smile on his face.

'Can you believe it?' he said softly.

Kartik grinned. 'We did it. We gave our village the power of the sun.'

As a gentle breeze rustled the leaves of the banyan tree, Kartik looked up at the sky.

'Thank you, Edmond Becquerel,' he whispered with a smile.

The sun had always been there, shining down on Rampur and its people. As always, everything people want usually presents itself at the right time.

All it had needed was someone to listen—and Kartik had done just that.

Rosalind Franklin

Discovery: DNA double helix (X-ray crystallography)

Rosalind Franklin was a British scientist who lived from 1920 to 1958. She made important discoveries in chemistry and biology, especially through her work with X-ray Crystallography—a method used to study the structure of molecules.

Franklin is best known for capturing an image known as Photo 51, which showed the double-helix shape of DNA. Her work provided a key piece of evidence that helped other scientists understand how DNA carries genetic information.

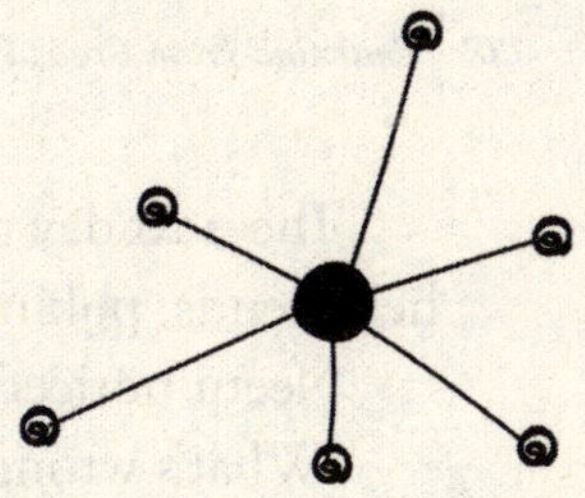

Nisha and the Science
of Bath Bombs

Nisha's kitchen was a disaster.

The floor was dusted with white powder, and streaks of food colouring stained the countertop. A large mixing bowl sat in the middle of the mess, filled with what should have been her latest batch of bath bombs.

Instead, the mixture sat there... a gloopy, half-fizzed mess.

'Not again!' Nisha groaned, dropping her spoon in frustration.

She had been trying to make bath bombs for Neetu's birthday. Her best friend loved long, relaxing baths, and Nisha had thought a batch of homemade fizzy bath bombs would be the perfect gift.

But this was her third failed attempt.

'Why is this so hard?' she muttered, staring at the clumpy mixture that refused to fizz properly.

The next day at school, Nisha sat in the cafeteria with her friends, poking at her lunch absentmindedly.

Neetu noticed her lack of enthusiasm.

'What's wrong, Nisha?' she asked, leaning closer.

'It's... nothing.' Nisha shrugged. But one look at Neetu's concerned expression, and the words tumbled out.

'I've been trying to make bath bombs for your birthday,' she confessed. 'But I can't get them right. They either crumble, don't fizz, or just turn into a weird paste!'

Neetu's eyes lit up.

'You're making me bath bombs?' she asked, touched.

'Well... I'm trying,' Nisha said, sighing. 'But it's not working. I don't know what I'm doing wrong.'

Mitul, who was sitting across from them, chimed in.

'You're playing with chemicals, Nisha,' he said, grinning. 'You need to know the science behind it.'

Nisha's eyes narrowed.

'Science? It's just baking soda and citric acid... how complicated can it be?'

'That's chemistry,' Mitul said, raising his eyebrows. 'If you want it to work, you need to get the balance right.'

'Chemistry...' Nisha murmured, her mind already spinning with ideas.

That evening, Nisha sat in her room, scrolling through websites about bath bombs.

'Baking soda and citric acid... when they mix with water, they create carbon dioxide... that's what makes the fizz...'

She read about pH levels, binding agents, and the role of essential oils. But what really caught her attention was a section about women pioneers in chemistry.

That's when she discovered Marie Curie and Rosalind Franklin.

'Marie Curie... the first woman to win a Nobel Prize. She discovered radium and polonium... and revolutionised the world of science.'

But it was Rosalind Franklin's work on the structure of DNA that fascinated Nisha the most.

'She used X-ray diffraction to capture images of DNA... and those images helped Watson and Crick understand the double helix.'

Nisha's eyes gleamed with inspiration.

'If they could uncover the secrets of atoms and DNA... I can figure out bath bombs!'

The next day, Nisha turned her kitchen into her own chemistry lab.

'Okay,' she said, tying her hair back and adjusting her apron. 'Time to apply some science.'

She carefully measured the baking soda and citric acid, making sure to get the ratio just right.

'1:2 ratio,' she murmured. 'That's what keeps the fizz going.'

She added cornstarch to slow down the reaction and Epsom salts for a soothing effect.

'Now, the binder...' Nisha thought aloud, adding a few drops of essential oils and witch hazel to hold the mixture together.

She pressed the mixture firmly into the molds, making sure there were no air gaps this time.

'No more crumbling,' she muttered.

Nisha's mom peeked into the kitchen, watching her daughter work with a look of quiet pride.

'What's all this, beta?' she asked.

'Science, Ma,' Nisha said with a grin. 'I'm making bath bombs using chemistry.'

Her mother smiled.

'You've been working so hard on this. I'm sure Neetu will love it.'

Nisha felt a wave of warmth wash over her.

'I hope so, Ma. This time... I think I've got it.'

After letting the bath bombs dry overnight, Nisha carefully popped one out of the mold.

'Perfect shape... no cracks...' she whispered, inspecting it closely.

She carried it to the bathroom, filled a bowl with warm water, and held her breath as she dropped the bath bomb in.

For a moment, nothing happened.

Then—

Fsssssssssssshhhhh!

The bath bomb fizzed beautifully, releasing tiny bubbles and a sweet lavender scent into the air.

Nisha's face lit up.

'Yes!' she shouted, pumping her fist. 'I did it!'

On Neetu's birthday, Nisha presented her with a neatly wrapped box.

'Happy Birthday, Neetu!' she said, her eyes twinkling with excitement.

Neetu tore off the wrapping paper and gasped when she saw what was inside.

'Bath bombs!' she squealed. 'You did it!'

'I finally figured it out,' Nisha said, beaming. 'I learned about chemistry... and some extraordinary women scientists who inspired me. It turns out making bath bombs is all about getting the science right.'

Neetu picked up one of the lavender-scented bombs, her eyes shining.

'I can't wait to try them!'

That evening, Neetu invited Nisha over to witness the grand test.

They filled the bathtub with warm water, and Neetu gently placed one of the bath bombs into the water.

Fsssshhhhhh...

The bomb dissolved perfectly, releasing a cascade of

fizz and a calming aroma into the air.

'This is great, Nisha!' Neetu sighed, sinking into the tub. 'It's perfect.'

Nisha sat on the edge of the tub, her heart swelling with pride.

'Happy Birthday, Neetu,' she said softly.

'This is the best gift ever,' Neetu murmured, her eyes closing as she relaxed in the soothing water.

In the days that followed, word spread about Nisha's homemade bath bombs.

'Can you make some for my mom?' Mitul asked.

'I'd love a batch for Diwali gifts!' another friend chimed in.

Nisha was thrilled.

'Maybe I can turn this into something bigger...' she thought, her mind racing with possibilities.

She had discovered a love for science and creativity, and with her newfound knowledge, she knew this was just the beginning.

'Marie Curie and Rosalind Franklin uncovered the mysteries of atoms and DNA,' Nisha murmured with a smile.

'And I... I've uncovered the perfect bath bomb.'

As she started experimenting with new scents and colours, Nisha realised that science wasn't just something she read about in books.

It was something she could use to create, discover, and make the world a little brighter—one bath bomb at a time.

Charles F Brush

Invention: Arc lamp; wind-powered generator

Charles F Brush was an American inventor and electrical engineer who lived from 1849 to 1929. He is best known for developing one of the first practical arc lamps, which produced bright light by creating an electric spark between two carbon rods.

His lighting system was used to illuminate streets, public buildings, and factories in the late 1800s, making cities safer and more active at night.

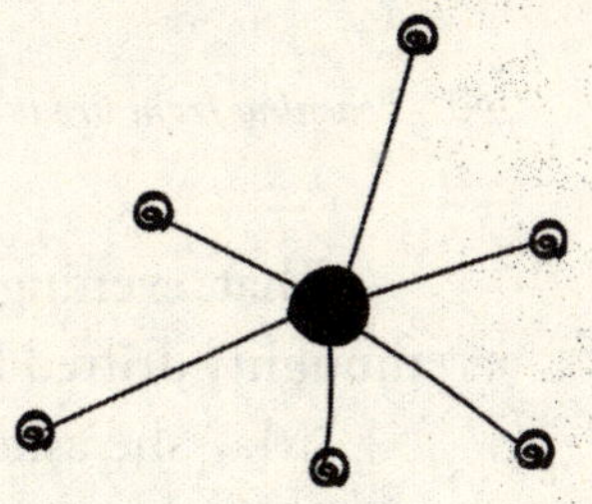

Ishita and the Power
of the Wind

Ishita stood at the edge of the beach, her hair whipping around her face as the wind howled past her. The waves crashed against the shore, and the salty air filled her lungs. She loved living in her coastal town of Devpur, where the breeze never seemed to rest.

But lately, Ishita had been thinking.

'The wind is so strong... it's always blowing,' she murmured, watching the palm trees sway. 'Isn't there a way we can use it?'

Her town often faced electricity shortages, and the community centre, where children gathered to read and study after school, was frequently plunged into darkness during power cuts.

'If only we could use the wind to power the lights,' Ishita thought, her mind already buzzing with possibilities.

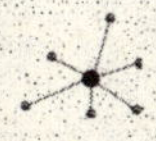

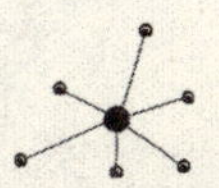

That evening, as Ishita sat at the dining table, her thoughts drifted back to the wind.

'Ma,' she asked, 'has anyone ever tried using wind to generate electricity?'

Her mother paused, looking thoughtful.

'I've heard about windmills that produce power,' she said. 'But that's something big cities do, beta. Not small towns like ours.'

Ishita frowned, her curiosity piqued.

'Maybe it's not impossible,' she murmured.

The next day, after school, Ishita rushed to the local library. She combed through books and articles, searching for information about wind energy.

That's when she stumbled upon the story of Charles F Brush.

'Charles Brush... built the first automatic wind turbine in 1888!' Ishita whispered, her eyes wide. 'He used it to power his home in Ohio... and it worked!'

Then, another story caught her eye—William Kamkwamba, a young boy from Malawi who had built a windmill from scrap materials to bring electricity to his village.

'If he could do it... so can I,' Ishita thought, determination sparking in her eyes.

The next morning, Ishita couldn't wait to tell her friends, Ravi and Ayesha, about her idea.

'A wind turbine?' Ravi asked, his eyebrows raised.

'To power the community centre?' Ayesha added, her eyes widening.

'Yes!' Ishita said, her excitement bubbling over. 'Think about it. The wind here is so strong. If we can build a small turbine, we can store enough energy to light up the centre during power cuts.'

Ravi scratched his head.

'But... do we know how to build one?'

'I've been reading about it,' Ishita said. 'We just need the right materials... and a little help.'

Over the next few days, the trio buried themselves in research.

'A wind turbine works by converting wind energy into electricity,' Ishita explained, flipping through her notebook. 'The wind spins the blades, which turn a rotor... that powers a generator.'

'And the generator produces electricity,' Ayesha added, her finger tracing a diagram they had found online.

'We'll need a motor, blades, and something to hold it all together,' Ravi said, jotting down notes.

'And batteries,' Ishita added. 'To store the energy for later use.'

They had a plan. Now, they just needed materials.

The trio scoured the junkyard behind the old factory, searching for useful parts.

'Look!' Ravi shouted, holding up an old bicycle wheel.

'Perfect for the rotor,' Ishita said, grinning.

Ayesha found PVC pipes that could be cut and shaped into blades.

'We'll need a small motor too,' she said, glancing around.

'Mr Sharma might have one,' Ravi suggested.

Mr Sharma, the village electrician, was intrigued when the children explained their plan.

'You want to build a wind turbine?' he asked, eyes twinkling.

'Yes, uncle,' Ishita said. 'We need a small motor to convert the energy.'

Mr Sharma rummaged through his toolbox and handed them an old DC motor.

'This should do the trick,' he said, smiling.

Under the shade of the banyan tree near the community centre, the children set to work.

'I'll cut the PVC pipes into blades,' Ravi said, carefully measuring and sawing.

'I'll attach the blades to the wheel,' Ayesha said, using strong adhesive to fix them securely.

Ishita focused on connecting the motor to the rotor and wiring it to a small battery.

'If this works,' she murmured, 'we'll have enough power to light up the centre.'

Hours of hard work later, their mini wind turbine was ready.

'Moment of truth,' Ravi said, wiping sweat from his forehead.

They carried the turbine to the roof of the community centre, where the wind was strongest.

'Ready?' Ishita asked, her heart pounding.

Ravi nodded, securing the turbine in place.

A gust of wind blew past, and the blades began to turn.

Slowly... then faster.

The rotor spun, and the motor whirred to life.

'It's working!' Ayesha cried, her eyes wide with excitement.

Ishita quickly checked the battery.

'The charge is building up,' she said, grinning. 'We're generating power!'

That evening, the children gathered at the community centre with Mr Sharma and some curious neighbours.

'We've been working on something,' Ishita said, her voice steady but excited.

Ravi connected the charged battery to the lights in the centre.

'Here goes,' he said, flipping the switch.

The room lit up.

A collective gasp echoed around them as the lights glowed brightly, powered by their small wind turbine.

'You did this?' Mrs Mehta, one of the village elders, asked in awe.

'We used the wind to generate electricity,' Ishita explained, beaming with pride.

Word spread quickly about Ishita and her friends' project.

'Can we build more turbines?' someone asked.

'Imagine if every rooftop had one!' another added.

With Mr Sharma's guidance and support from the community, they began building more turbines, improving their design each time.

'Charles F Brush and William Kamkwamba inspired me,' Ishita said one evening as she watched the turbines spinning in the wind. 'Now, we're helping our village too.'

Ravi grinned.

'And all because you wondered if the wind could do more than just blow.'

Ayesha smiled, her eyes on the glowing lights of the community centre.

'Who knew the wind could bring so much light?'

As the breeze whispered through the trees, Ishita looked up at the sky.

'Thank you, wind,' she murmured softly.

In her heart, she knew this was just the beginning.

William Perkin

Invention: Synthetic dye (mauve)

William Perkin was a British chemist who lived from 1838 to 1907. He is best known for accidentally discovering the first synthetic dye, called mauve, when he was just 18 years old.

While trying to create a medicine to treat malaria, he noticed that one of his experiments produced a bright purple colour. At the time, purple dye was rare and expensive, so his discovery quickly became popular in the fashion world.

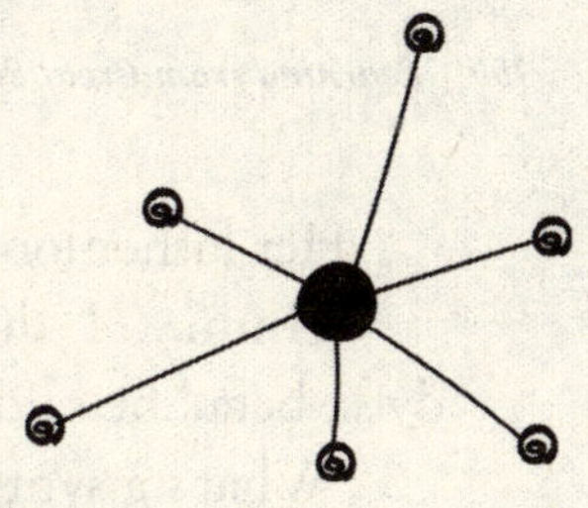

Rhea and the Magic of Colours

Rhea loved to paint. Her room was filled with canvases splashed in vibrant shades of blue, red, and yellow. Bottles of paint lined her desk, and her hands were almost always stained with a rainbow of colours.

But one afternoon, as she sat mixing shades of green for her latest painting, a thought struck her.

'Where do these colours come from?' she murmured, swirling her brush in the palette.

The bright pigments blended beautifully, but Rhea's mind was elsewhere.

'Paint comes in tubes and bottles... but how do they make the colours?'

That evening, during dinner, Rhea couldn't hold back her questions any longer.

'Papa,' she asked, 'do you know how paints get their colours?'

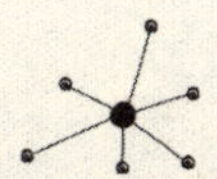

Her father looked up from his plate, surprised.

'Hmm... I think most paints today use synthetic dyes, beta,' he said.

'What's a synthetic dye?' Rhea frowned.

'It's a man-made chemical that gives colour,' her father explained. 'But a long time ago, people used natural materials to make dyes—things like plants, flowers, and even insects.'

Rhea's eyes widened.

'Natural dyes?'

Her father smiled.

'Yes. In fact, the first synthetic dye was discovered by accident by a man named Sir William Perkin.'

Rhea couldn't stop thinking about her father's words. The next day, she rushed to the school library and asked the librarian, Mrs D'Souza, for help.

'You want to know about William Perkin?' Mrs D'Souza's eyes twinkled. 'He's quite an interesting figure in history.'

She led Rhea to the science section and handed her a book.

As Rhea flipped through the pages, she read about how Perkin was only 18 years old when he made his discovery.

'He was trying to create a medicine for malaria... but by accident, he ended up with a purple substance instead,' Rhea murmured, fascinated.

The book described how Perkin's purple dye, later named mauveine, became the first synthetic dye and revolutionised the textile industry.

'A mistake that changed the world,' Rhea whispered, her mind racing with ideas.

Inspired by Perkin's story, Rhea decided she wanted to experiment with natural dyes.

That weekend, she told her best friends, Tanya and Arjun, about her idea.

'I want to make my own dyes,' she said, her eyes gleaming with excitement.

'Dyes? From what?' Tanya asked, curious.

'Plants, fruits... whatever I can find,' Rhea replied. 'I read that people used turmeric, beetroot, and even flowers to make colours.'

'That sounds cool!' Arjun said, already intrigued.

'But what will you do with the dyes?' Tanya asked.

'Paint with them!' Rhea grinned. 'I'm going to create a special art project for the school exhibition.'

The trio spent the next few days collecting materials.

'Turmeric for yellow,' Rhea said, holding up the bright yellow spice.

'Beetroot for red,' Arjun added, pulling out a bunch of fresh beets.

'And hibiscus flowers for pink,' Tanya chimed in, her hands full of vibrant petals.

They also gathered spinach leaves for green and blueberries for purple.

'This is going to be fun,' Rhea said, her excitement growing with every ingredient they collected.

Rhea transformed her kitchen into a makeshift lab.

'Okay,' she said, tying her apron and pulling her hair back. 'Time to make some colours!'

She boiled the beetroot and watched as the water turned a deep red.

'This looks so cool!' Arjun exclaimed.

Tanya mashed the hibiscus petals, releasing a rich pink juice.

'It smells so good,' she said, smiling.

Rhea ground the turmeric and mixed it with water, producing a bright yellow liquid.

One by one, they extracted the colours, letting the natural dyes cool and settle.

'These are beautiful,' Rhea murmured, holding up small jars filled with vibrant hues.

Rhea grabbed a piece of cloth and dipped it into the beetroot dye.

'Look at that red!' she said, her face lighting up.

They tested the other dyes, and soon, their workspace was filled with pieces of fabric dyed in shades of pink, yellow, green, and purple.

'We did it!' Tanya cheered.

'Now,' Rhea said with a grin, 'it's time to paint.'

For the next few days, Rhea worked tirelessly on her painting for the school exhibition.

She used the natural dyes to paint a breathtaking landscape—a vibrant sunset where the sky blended shades of orange, pink, and purple, and the ground was filled with flowers in hues of yellow, red, and green.

'This is great, Rhea,' Arjun said, watching her add the finishing touches.

'It's like the colours are alive,' Tanya whispered, admiring the rich tones.

The day of the school exhibition finally arrived.

Rhea's painting stood proudly in the centre of the hall, its colours glowing under the lights. A small card next to it read:

'Painted with Nature: Exploring the World of Natural Dyes.'

Crowds gathered around her artwork, amazed by the vibrant colours.

'You made these colours yourself?' Mrs D'Souza asked, her eyes twinkling with pride.

'Yes, ma'am,' Rhea said, beaming. 'I was inspired by William Perkin's discovery of the first synthetic dye, but

I wanted to explore how colours were made before that... from nature.'

Mrs D'Souza nodded, impressed.

'You've not only created a beautiful piece of art, Rhea,' she said softly, 'but you've also brought science and creativity together. That's truly remarkable.'

After the exhibition, Rhea's project caught the attention of her science teacher, Mr Kapoor.

'Rhea, would you like to lead a workshop on natural dyes for the younger classes?' he asked.

Rhea's eyes lit up.

'I'd love that, sir!' she said eagerly.

As she stood beside her colourful masterpiece, Rhea realised that her journey of curiosity had led her to something much bigger than she had ever imagined.

She had discovered the magic of colours—a blend of art, science, and nature.

And this was just the beginning.

'Thank you, Sir William Perkin,' Rhea whispered with a smile.

She couldn't wait to see where her love for colours would take her next.

Euclid
Foundations of geometry (Elements)

Euclid was an ancient Greek mathematician who lived around 300 BCE and is often called the Father of Geometry. He worked in Alexandria, Egypt, and wrote a famous book called *Elements,* which collected and organised all the known knowledge of geometry at the time.

Elements became one of the most important and widely used textbooks in history and was studied for over 2,000 years.

Himani's Geometric Gift

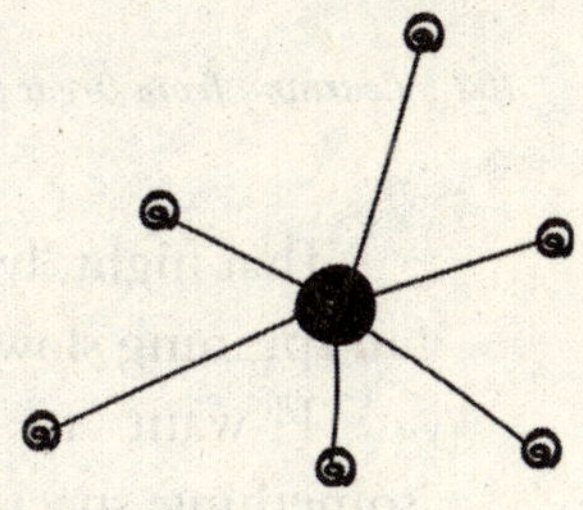

The air in the house was full of excitement and something else—nervousness. Himani sat cross-legged on her bed, watching her older sister, Kangana, fold her clothes into a neatly packed suitcase.

'Do you really have to go?' Himani asked, her voice small.

Kangana smiled and nodded. 'It's just boarding school, Himani. I'll come home for holidays. And I'll call you all the time!'

'I'll miss you every single day,' Himani murmured.

Kangana came over and hugged her tightly. 'I'll miss you too. But I'm going to learn new things and make new friends. It's a big step for me.'

Himani knew Kangana was brave—but she could also tell that her sister was nervous underneath that confident smile.

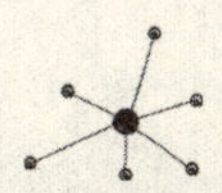

That night, lying in bed, Himani stared at the ceiling fan spinning slowly above her.

'I want to give her something,' she thought, 'something special. Something that will remind her of home—and of me.'

But what?

The next morning in school, during math class, Mr Sharma was introducing a new topic.

'Class, today we begin a journey into geometry, starting with the foundations laid by a great mathematician—Euclid.'

Himani's ears perked up.

'Euclid lived in ancient Greece,' Mr Sharma continued. 'His book, *Elements*, is one of the most important mathematical texts in history. He showed how you can build complex shapes using just a straightedge and a compass—two simple tools.'

He drew a perfect circle on the board. 'Everything starts with this.'

As Himani watched lines and shapes appear on the blackboard, an idea began to take root in her mind.

'What if I make something using geometry? Something beautiful... and full of meaning. Kangana would love that!'

During lunch, Himani turned to her best friend, Babita.

'Babu, I need your help,' she whispered.

Babita leaned in, curious. 'What's going on?'

'I want to make a special gift for Kangana before she

leaves. I want to use geometry—like what Mr Sharma showed us today.'

Babita's eyes lit up. 'That sounds amazing! But how do we even start?'

'We'll go to the library after school,' Himani said, determined. 'We need to learn more about Euclid and how to actually draw the shapes.'

Babita grinned. 'You had me at "special project." Let's do it!'

The two girls spent their afternoon in the school library. They found a book titled *Geometry Through the Ages* and flipped to the chapter about Euclid's Elements.

'Here!' Himani pointed. 'It says Euclid began with five postulates, or rules. Using those, he showed how to construct all sorts of shapes.'

Babita read aloud: 'With a compass and straightedge, you can draw perfect circles, bisect angles, and create triangles and hexagons...'

'I love this!' Himani exclaimed. 'It's like building a puzzle where every step matters.'

They took notes, sketched diagrams, and practiced drawing circles, lines, and angles. Himani's notebook quickly filled with attempts—some crooked, some smudged—but improving every time.

'We're getting better,' Babita said proudly.

'We'll be Euclid-level experts in no time!' Himani giggled.

Back at home, Himani spread her notes across the dining table. She and Babita had decided on the perfect project: a geometric mandala.

'Each shape can represent something,' Himani explained. 'Like a circle for family, a triangle for strength, and stars for dreams. It'll be like a secret message just for Kangana.'

Babita nodded. 'And we'll use colours she loves—lavender and sky blue.'

They gathered their tools: a compass, a straightedge, pencil, eraser, watercolour paints, and thick ivory paper.

They marked the centre and drew the first circle, then six more, each touching the previous one—forming the ancient pattern known as the Seed of Life.

'This pattern has been around since ancient times,' Himani whispered, admiring the symmetry. 'Just like Euclid said—it all starts with a circle.'

Over the next few evenings, Himani and Babita built layer upon layer of patterns: equilateral triangles, interlocking hexagons, curved petals, and stars. Each line was made with precision, measured and constructed by the rules of Euclidean geometry.

'This triangle here,' Himani said one night, 'this one's for courage. Because Kangana is brave to go somewhere new.'

'Then this circle can be for home,' Babita added, drawing it carefully. 'Because no matter how far she goes, she'll always be connected to us.'

They painted the shapes with soft watercolours, careful not to blur the edges.

The mandala began to glow with harmony and colour, a balance of science and art.

As they worked, Himani began to see how geometry was more than just lines and angles.

'It's a language,' she told Babita. 'It's about logic— one step leads to the next. But it's also about beauty, like how everything fits perfectly when it's done right.'

Babita smiled. 'It's like life, in a way. One thing builds on another. And sometimes, the most beautiful things come from simple rules.'

They decided to name their project '*The Geometry of Us.*'

The night before Kangana was to leave, Himani placed the mandala in a simple wooden frame and wrapped it with recycled paper and string.

She tucked a handwritten note behind it:

Dear Kangana,

This mandala is made using the same tools ancient mathematicians used—just a compass and a straightedge. Every shape is chosen with love. Every line connects to you. When you feel nervous, look at this and remember: you are strong, you are loved, and you're never alone.

Love,

Himani (and Babita too!)

The next morning, just before the taxi arrived, Himani handed Kangana the wrapped frame.

'A gift?' Kangana asked, surprised.

'Open it when you're settled,' Himani said with a shy smile. 'It's something I made. With help from Babita.'

Kangana hugged her tightly. 'I will. Thank you, little one.'

A week later, Himani received a video message.

On the screen, Kangana sat on her dorm bed, the framed mandala hanging on the wall behind her.

'I opened it the night I arrived,' she said, her eyes misty. 'It's the most beautiful thing I've ever received. Every time I look at it, I feel like you're right here with me. I even showed it to my new roommate—she said it looked like something a professional artist made.'

She laughed. 'But I told her, no—it's something a genius little sister and her amazing best friend made.'

From that day on, Himani found herself looking at

math differently. Geometry wasn't just a school subject—it was a way to express herself. It was logic turned into love, precision transformed into art.

And every time she picked up her compass and straightedge, she remembered how something as simple as a shape could hold a world of meaning.

Jacques Cousteau

Invention: Aqua-Lung; ocean exploration and conservation

Jacques Cousteau was a French explorer, filmmaker, and marine biologist who lived from 1910 to 1997. He is best known for his deep love of the ocean and for helping people all over the world learn about life under the sea. Cousteau co-invented the Aqua-Lung, an early type of scuba gear that allowed divers to stay underwater for long periods. This invention opened up a whole new world of exploration beneath the waves.

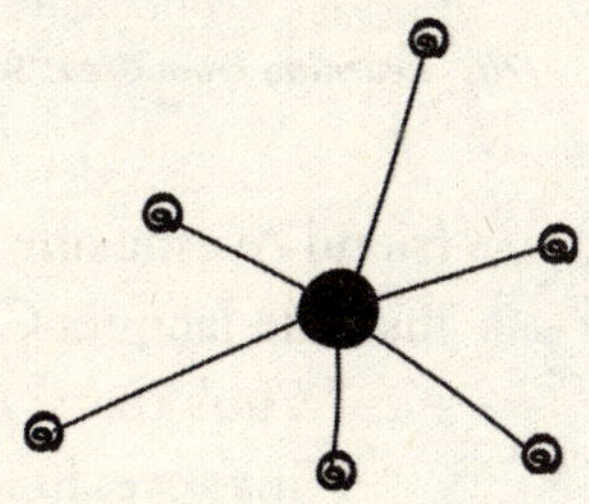

Nina and the Deep-Sea Dream

Nina loved swimming more than anything in the world. Her parents often joked that she must've been a mermaid in a past life. Every chance she got—whether it was at the beach or the community pool—she dove right in, swimming smooth and fast like a dolphin.

But more than just swimming, Nina was fascinated by what lived *under* the water. Fish that shimmered like jewels, coral reefs in strange, beautiful shapes, and mysterious sea creatures that glowed in the deep dark ocean—all of it felt magical.

She kept a scrapbook filled with pictures of sea turtles, jellyfish, and submarine landscapes. Her room was full of seashells, ocean posters, and a blue light that made her ceiling look like waves at night.

'I want to see it for real someday,' she said to her

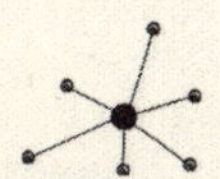

friend Ayesha one afternoon. 'I want to explore the ocean just like Jacques Cousteau.'

'Who's that?' Ayesha asked.

Nina's eyes lit up. 'He was a famous undersea explorer! He helped invent the Aqua-Lung so people could breathe underwater. He made movies and books about the sea, and he spent his life protecting it.'

Ayesha smiled. 'Sounds like a cool guy.'

'The coolest,' Nina said, already opening her Cousteau biography to show her friend a photo of him in his red cap, standing on the deck of his ship, *Calypso*.

That night, Nina couldn't stop thinking about Cousteau. She read about how he had always been curious, just like her, and how his inventions helped people dive deeper than ever before.

'What if I made something too?' she wondered aloud. 'Something that makes me feel like I'm a deep-sea diver, right here on land?'

She flipped open her notebook and started sketching. A helmet! Not a real diving helmet with metal and air tanks—that would be dangerous—but a *pretend* one. A safe, creative version that could simulate what it *felt* like to explore underwater.

And even better, she could use it to teach her classmates about ocean life—and how important it was to protect it.

The next weekend, Nina and her dad headed to the recycling centre. They picked up a clear plastic salad bowl, an old backpack, some tubing from an old toy vacuum,

and colourful plastic bits and stickers.

Back home, Nina got to work. With her parents' help (and plenty of hot glue and duct tape), she built a pretend diving helmet. The clear bowl became the main part of the helmet, with the vacuum tubes acting like pretend air hoses that looped down into the backpack.

She painted fish and coral on the outside and added a paper dial that said 'Depth Level: Shallow / Mid / Deep.' Her mom helped her cut holes in the backpack and stuff it with soft cotton to keep it lightweight. She even added a mini flashlight to the side, like a real diver might use to see in the dark.

When she wore it and stood in front of her mirror, she gasped. She looked like a tiny ocean explorer!

'I shall name this,' she said dramatically, 'The Sea Explorer Mark I!'

The next day at school, Nina asked her science

teacher, Mr Jain, if she could do a presentation.

'I want to talk about Jacques Cousteau and the ocean,' she said. 'And I made something too.'

Mr Jain smiled. 'You've got my curiosity. Let's schedule it for Friday's science period.'

Nina spent the whole week preparing. She made colourful posters of coral reefs and endangered sea creatures. She printed facts about Cousteau's inventions and added big, bold letters that said: Protect Our Oceans!

She also researched ocean pollution—plastic waste, oil spills, overfishing—and how they were harming the creatures she loved so much. She added a new section to her presentation: *What You Can Do to Help*.

On Friday, Nina walked into the classroom carrying her helmet and posters. She wore a blue T-shirt with a picture of a dolphin and had waves painted on her cheeks.

The room went quiet as she placed the Sea Explorer Mark I on her head and turned on the tiny flashlight. Everyone stared.

'Hello, crew!' she said in a dramatic voice. 'Today, I'm diving into the deep sea to share the story of one of the greatest ocean explorers—Jacques Cousteau!'

She explained how Cousteau had loved the sea, how he'd helped invent equipment that let people breathe underwater, and how he'd made films to show the world what lived below the surface.

'But the ocean is in trouble,' she said, holding up a poster with a sea turtle tangled in plastic. 'Millions of tons of plastic are dumped into the ocean every year. It's hurting fish, birds, turtles—even coral reefs!'

The class looked solemn.

'But there's hope,' Nina said. 'We can help. Use less plastic. Recycle. Say no to plastic straws. Join a beach cleanup. Every little bit makes a difference.'

She ended with a bow, and the class burst into applause.

Mr Jain beamed. 'That was fantastic, Nina. You didn't just build something—you made us *think*.'

Over the next few days, something amazing happened.

Kids in school started bringing reusable bottles and lunchboxes. The cafeteria stopped using plastic straws. And Mr Jain even put up a sign on the science board: *OCEAN HERO OF THE MONTH: NINA.*

Ayesha came up to her at lunch. 'You know what I loved most? That you made something fun *and* useful. I want to build something too! Maybe a robot that picks up trash?'

'Yes!' Nina grinned. 'We could even make it float in water!'

As a surprise, Nina's parents took her to the city aquarium. There, she saw live jellyfish, watched sea otters play, and even stood in a glass tunnel while sharks swam overhead.

But what excited her most was a special exhibit called *The Legacy of Jacques Cousteau*. It had photos, videos, and even a replica of the Aqua-Lung.

'I know him!' Nina told the guide. 'He inspired my project at school!'

The guide smiled. 'Then you're carrying on his

mission. That's what he always wanted—people who love the ocean and want to protect it.'

Back home, Nina placed her helmet on a shelf with her seashells and ocean books. But her mind was already racing.

'Maybe I can build a working submarine model next,' she whispered. 'Or start a club at school for ocean lovers.'

Her dad overheard and laughed. 'One Jacques Cousteau at a time, okay?'

Nina grinned. 'Okay. But he'd want me to dream big.'
And so she did.

James Watt

Improved steam engine

James Watt was a Scottish inventor and engineer who lived from 1736 to 1819. He is best known for improving the steam engine, making it much more efficient and practical for use in factories, mines, and transportation.

Although he didn't invent the steam engine itself, his improvements—like adding a separate condenser—greatly increased its power and reduced fuel use.

This helped spark the Industrial Revolution, a period of major change when machines began to replace manual labour.

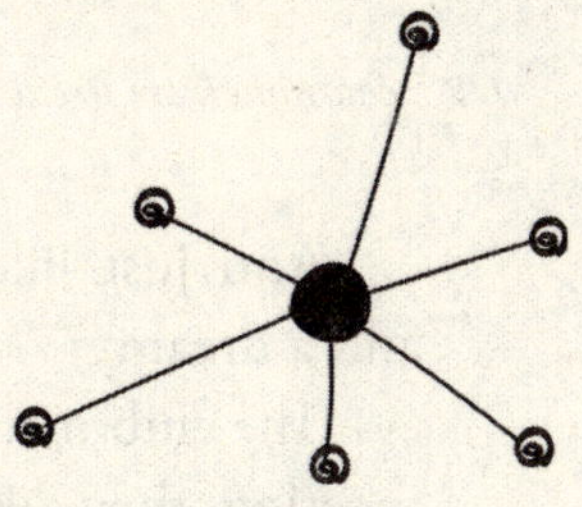

The Backyard Science Club

The shed in Varun's backyard had always been a dusty little place where old tools and forgotten boxes lived. But to Varun and his three best friends—Rahul, Kalpesh, and Jitendra—it was about to become something much more exciting.

'I'm telling you,' Varun said one hot afternoon, sweeping cobwebs out of the corners, 'we can turn this into our very own science lab!'

Kalpesh looked around the small wooden room. 'You really think we can pull that off?'

'Why not?' said Rahul, already bringing in some stools. 'We've got space, curiosity, and four brains. That's enough to start something awesome.'

'We'll call it... the Backyard Science Club!' Jitendra shouted.

And just like that, the boys had a name, a place, and a dream.

The club met every Saturday after lunch. On the first meeting, they decided on the rules: they would pick one famous scientist each week, learn about their life and discoveries, and try to recreate one of their experiments in a fun, kid-safe way.

'Let's start with someone big,' said Kalpesh. 'Like... James Watt!'

Rahul nodded. 'He made the steam engine more powerful and efficient, right?'

'Exactly,' said Varun, opening up his school tablet. 'His improvements helped power factories, trains, and even changed how the world worked during the Industrial Revolution.'

'So what are we building?' Jitendra asked, grinning. 'A train?'

'Not quite,' Varun said. 'But we can make a mini steam engine using a soda can, some water, and a candle!'

The next Saturday, the boys brought their materials: empty cans, string, plastic bottle caps, candles, and safety gloves. They had read all about James Watt's innovations and were ready to give their experiment a try.

Under adult supervision, they filled a soda can with a little water, poked two holes on the sides with bent straws, and placed it over a candle's flame on a stand. Slowly, steam began to hiss from the straws—and the can started to spin!

'It works!' Jitendra cheered. 'We made a steam turbine!'

'Just like Watt improved the original idea of a steam engine,' said Rahul. 'Except ours runs on soda and science.'

They high-fived each other, already eager for the next week.

The second scientist they studied was Galileo Galilei.

'He proved that objects fall at the same speed, no matter their weight,' Kalpesh explained, reading from a library book. 'And he discovered how pendulums move.'

So for their experiment, the club set up a pendulum using a piece of string and a washer. They timed how long it took to swing back and forth.

Then they changed the weight at the end and tried again.

'The weight doesn't matter—it still swings the same!' Varun said in amazement.

'Galileo figured this out by watching a swinging lamp in church,' said Jitendra. 'I guess science can start anywhere.'

Word about the Backyard Science Club began to spread. Some classmates started asking if they could watch or help. The boys decided to let others visit during special "science showcase" days.

Meanwhile, every Saturday brought a new adventure.

One week, Rahul suggested they study a scientist who wasn't just a man. 'Let's learn about Marie Curie, the first woman to win a Nobel Prize—and she won it twice!'

'She discovered radium and polonium, and helped invent X-rays,' said Kalpesh. 'But radioactive stuff is dangerous. We can't touch that.'

So they found a safe chemistry experiment instead—making glowing liquids using tonic water and a black light.

They learned how quinine, a compound in tonic water, glows under ultraviolet light—like how Curie discovered glowing elements!

'It's like a safe version of radiation,' said Varun, as the club's darkened shed lit up with soft blue glow.

When it was Jitendra's turn to pick a scientist, he chose Albert Einstein.

'We can't exactly recreate relativity,' Rahul said.

'True,' Jitendra agreed. 'But we can learn about how light moves—and maybe make a periscope!'

Using mirrors and cardboard tubes, they made simple periscopes to explore the bending of light.

'Einstein taught us to always ask "why,"' said Varun. 'That's what science is really about—being curious.'

They stuck a sign on the wall of their shed: *Curiosity is more important than knowledge – Albert Einstein.*

Not everything went smoothly. One week, their experiment using baking soda and vinegar to inflate a balloon failed because someone forgot the funnel. Another week, they accidentally spilled cornstarch everywhere while making oobleck for an Isaac Newton experiment.

'Science is messy,' Kalpesh said, mopping up the goop. 'Just like real life.'

'And we learn more from mistakes anyway,' Rahul added.

They kept going—cleaning, laughing, trying again.

When they studied Nikola Tesla, they tried to make

a simple motor with a battery, a magnet, and a coil. It didn't work at first.

'I don't get it!' Jitendra frowned. 'We followed the steps exactly.'

They sat in silence for a while. Then Varun said, 'Tesla failed a lot too. But he kept going until things worked.'

They checked their connections and realised the coil had to be just the right size. After a few adjustments—success!

The tiny wire started spinning slowly.

'Our own electric motor,' Rahul whispered in awe.

Their science teacher, Ms Meena, heard about the club and visited one day.

'You've created something wonderful here,' she said, admiring their experiment wall full of diagrams, notes, and sketches. 'Would you boys like to represent the school at the District Science Fair?'

The club members exchanged wide-eyed looks.

'Us? Really?'

'Absolutely,' she said. 'You've shown curiosity, teamwork, and real scientific thinking.'

They decided to present their "Mini Scientist of the Week" concept, demonstrating simplified versions of the steam engine, pendulum, glowing liquids, and their periscope.

The fair was packed with visitors, but the Backyard Science Club's booth stood out. Kids and parents gathered around, fascinated by how science could be made fun and hands-on.

They didn't win the top prize—but they did win something special: the "Young Innovators Award." And even better, they inspired a few other students to start their own clubs.

Back at the shed the next week, Rahul said, 'So… who's next week's scientist?'

Varun smiled. 'How about William Kamkwamba?'

Kalpesh's eyes lit up. 'The boy who built a windmill from scraps in Malawi?'

'Yes!' said Jitendra. 'Let's try building our own tiny wind turbine!'

The friends huddled together, sketching ideas on the back of an old cereal box. The shed was filled with the sound of imagination, curiosity, and friendship.

And outside, the wind rustled the leaves—ready to power their next big idea.